Birds and the War
Messenger Pigeons and other Birds During World War One

by Hugh Gladstone

with an introduction by Jackson Chambers

This work contains material that was originally published in 1919.

This publication is within the Public Domain.

This edition is reprinted for educational purposes and in accordance with all applicable Federal Laws.

Introduction Copyright 2017 by Jackson Chambers

Self Reliance Books

Get more historic titles on animal and stock breeding, gardening and old fashioned skills by visiting us at:

http://selfreliancebooks.blogspot.com/

Introduction

I am pleased to present yet another title in the "Pigeons" series.

This volume is entitled "Birds in the War" and was published in 1919.

The work is in the Public Domain and is re-printed here in accordance with Federal Laws.

As with all reprinted books of this age that are intended to perfectly reproduce the original edition, considerable pains and effort had to be undertaken to correct fading and sometimes outright damage to existing proofs of this title. At times, this task is quite monumental, requiring an almost total "rebuilding" of some pages from digital proofs of multiple copies. Despite this, imperfections still sometimes exist in the final proof and may detract from the visual appearance of the text.

I hope you enjoy reading this book as much as I enjoyed making it available to readers again.

Jackson Chambers

Foreword

"You call them thieves and pillagers; but know
 They are the wingèd wardens of your farms,
Who from the cornfields drive the insidious foe,
 And from your harvests keep a hundred harms."

LONGFELLOW.

PREFACE

ON the outbreak of the European War in 1914 I made up my mind to collect all the information I could regarding its effects upon the life of Birds. The result has been the accumulation of a large collection of cuttings, from scientific publications as well as newspapers, and it has been with no little difficulty that this has been collated. I regret that none of my information has been derived at first hand; my military duties kept me in London, but "the looker-on sees most of the game," and there is no doubt that my position gave me exceptional facilities, which otherwise I might not have had, for accumulating the mass of notes now at my disposal.

The subject of Birds and the War is one which it is hoped will one day be tackled scientifically and internationally. It has been already considered in Russia by the Petro-

Preface

grad Society of Naturalists under Mr. D. M. Rossinsky and Professor D. N. Kaigorodov; in France by MM. Cunisset-Carnot, Reboussin, and Edmond Perrier; in Germany by Veterinary Surgeon Dr. Reuter; in America by Dr. Arthur Allan, head of Cornell University; and probably other authorities, of whom I am unaware, have contributed to the subject. I can claim nothing original for my observations; the majority of the notes I quote appeared anonymously in newspapers, but some are by recognised authorities such as Messrs. Charles Dixon, A. H. Patterson, Thoburn Clarke, Oliver G. Pike, and Miss E. L. Turner.

For lack of better arrangement I have arranged my notes in five chapters, divided again into twelve sections, which seem more or less to cover the subject as I have dealt with it. There are, however, some ramifications which remain untraced and it has been impossible to utilise all of my notes. For example, when writing of the utility of birds, I have omitted to state that the New Zealand Government sent a quantity of SWANS' quills,

Preface

with appropriate paintings thereon, to be sold for the benefit of the Belgian Relief Fund at 1s. and 2s. 6d. each. Nor have I mentioned cases in which spies carried on apparently harmless correspondence, using the names of birds, fish, and animals to denote airships, submarines, and other engines of war. Again birds figured largely in the cartoons which appeared from time to time in the comic papers. They played their part also in the auctions which were held throughout the country on behalf of "war charities"; in August 1918 it was announced that the famous Warboys (Huntingdonshire) COCKEREL had raised £12,762 for the Red Cross. In three years he had travelled 17,300 miles, had been sold 10,960 times, and had made close on fifty times his weight in gold (*Daily Express*, 30.viii.18). Naturally the war caused no little stir in our scientific societies, in which there was bound to be a proportion of alien, if not enemy, members, and it may safely be said that no society took up this question more hotly than the British Ornithologists' Union; the annual general meetings

Preface

of 1917 and 1918 were so stormy that they are not likely to be soon forgotten by any member who was present. Ramifications such as these I have indicated show that the subjects of Birds and the War might be prolonged to infinity; my method of dealing with it makes no claim to finality. Had I extended the range of my notes to include the effect of the war on Animals, Reptiles, and Insects, I might have recorded many strange stories; but none more remarkable than that of the frogs in the marshy Aillette district, which are alleged, when the Germans were preparing to storm the Chemins des Dames, to have croaked so vociferously that they enabled the enemy to bring up their batteries and ammunition columns without discovery, whilst when the attack was actually launched the frogs' deafening concert prevented the location of the hostile machine guns (*Lokalanzeiger*, 3.vii.18). I have, however, tried to keep within the limits prescribed by my title—BIRDS AND THE WAR.

This introduction will explain the conception of my work in which I am aware that

Preface

much is lacking. It is obvious that its publication is premature until the whole subject can be studied internationally. For instance, the real economic conditions prevalent in Germany are as yet so imperfectly known that it is impossible to assess the value placed on birds as food; the legislation affecting them is unknown, and must remain so until a period of peace has elapsed sufficient to safeguard the revelation of this secret as of no military value. The German, Austrian, and other enemy journals have not been accessible, and doubtless much information could be obtained by a careful scrutiny of our Allies' scientific publications such as the *Revue Française d'Ornithologie*, etc. Now that the embargo on the disclosure of certain military details, previously regarded as secret, has been removed, and with the return home of many soldiers from the front, information on the subject of "Birds and the War" is only now being brought to light.

Fully realising that my work is but an imperfect sketch of the finished picture, I have been careful to give references for all my

Preface

statements so that they may at least prove of assistance to any one who may hereafter work up the subject as it deserves. I had hoped to delay the publication of my book until after the declaration of peace, when I might have had leisure to sift and to elaborate my notes, but this hope has been frustrated by the knowledge that more important work will then confront me; I have therefore felt compelled to publish them as they now stand.

I must thank my friend Captain Harold Stannard for his assistance in preparing my notes for publication and also for reading the proofs of the book. As regards the pictures and photographs which I have been enabled to reproduce as illustrations, I am indebted to the courtesy of the Imperial War Museum (Photographic Section) for Plates 1, 2, 7, 8, 12, 13, 15, 16, and 17; to the Canadian War Records Office for Plates 3 and 4; to the Associated Illustration Agencies, Ltd., for Plate 5; to Mr. F. W. Frohawk and the Editor of *The Field* for Plate 6; to the Alfieri Picture Service for Plate 9; to the London Electrotype Agency, Ltd., for

Preface

Plate 14; to Miss Estella Canziani, the French War Emergency Fund, and the Medici Society, Ltd., for Plate 10; and to Newspaper Illustrations, Ltd., for Plate 11.

HUGH S. GLADSTONE.

40 LENNOX GARDENS, S.W.1.
April 1919.

CONTENTS

I. UTILITY AND ECONOMY OF BIRDS IN THE WAR

                                              PAGE

1. BIRDS AS MESSENGERS . . . 3
2. BIRDS AS CROP PROTECTORS . . 29
3. BIRDS AS FOOD 42
4. BIRDS' EGGS AS FOOD . . . 60

II. SUFFERINGS OF BIRDS IN THE WAR

5. EFFECT OF THE WAR ON BIRDS IN CAPTIVITY, AND DURING SEVERE WEATHER 67
6. DESTRUCTION OF BIRDS AT SEA . 75
7. EFFECT OF AIR-RAIDS AND AIR-CRAFT ON BIRDS . . . 80

Contents

III. BEHAVIOUR OF BIRDS IN THE WAR ZONES

	PAGE
8. BIRDS ON THE WESTERN FRONT	99
9. BIRDS ON THE GALLIPOLI, ITALIAN, MACEDONIAN, PALESTINE, AND MESOPOTAMIAN FRONTS	135

IV. EFFECT OF THE WAR ON BIRDS

10. MIGRATION IN WAR-TIME	143
11. CHANGE OF HABITS IN BIRDS DUE TO THE WAR	154

V. CONCLUSION

12. ORNITHOLOGISTS KILLED IN THE WAR	165

LIST OF ILLUSTRATIONS

PLATE
1. "An EAGLE ... became the pet of a subaltern" . . . . *Frontispiece*

FACING PAGE
2. "Our Military Pigeon Service ... grew to large proportions" 8

3. "The PIGEONS were taken, by bicyclists, in wicker crates to the front-line trenches" 9

4. "PIGEONS ... proved of the greatest use; particularly when the telegraph and telephone wires had been cut by shell fire" . 16

5. "HOMERS were taken up in aeroplanes, and 'tossed' with messages from behind the German lines" 17

6. "Had the feat of this PIGEON been performed by a human being, it might well have been rewarded by the V.C." 32

7. "Although hundreds of CANARIES were killed by our shell and gas, those that were rescued ... were ... well cared for" . 33

List of Illustrations

PLATE		FACING PAGE
8.	"CANARIES were ... used in ambulance trains to cheer our wounded soldiers with their sweet song"	48
9.	"The first woman gamekeeper"	48
10.	"A wounded soldier ... feeding the GULLS"	49
11.	"A bird hostel, where soldiers' pet birds were received"	80
12.	"A landscape of shattered trees and the ground so torn up by shells that there scarcely remained a single blade of grass"	81
13.	"To go up the communication trenches is like a ramble down a country lane"	81
14.	"SWALLOWS quietly perched on war-telegraph wires"	112
15.	"A pet MAGPIE ... found in the German trenches"	113
16.	"A PIGEON ... accompanied the guns through several fights"	144
17.	"A STORK ... acquired the habit of meeting our aeroplanes"	145

I—UTILITY AND ECONOMY OF BIRDS IN THE WAR

B

1—BIRDS AS MESSENGERS

IN the "Pigeon Post" we have the most obvious example of service rendered to man by birds during the war. The HOMING PIGEON, whose speed of flight has been estimated at from 880 to 2,000 yards per minute according to weather conditions, has naturally played an important part. The first use of PIGEONS as message carriers is wrapped in the mystery of antiquity. Solomon is alleged to have transmitted orders throughout his kingdom by means of HOMING PIGEONS, the ancient Greeks, Egyptians, and Romans employed these birds in their armies, and the victory at the siege of Modena (43 B.C.) has been attributed to PIGEONS. After the conquest of Gaul, relays of PIGEONS carried the news to Rome, as, in later days, the news of the victory at Waterloo was brought to England by PIGEONS some days in advance of the official courier (*Country Life*,

4.i.19). In the Franco-Prussian War of 1870 they were extensively used, and in the South African War of 1899–1902 they were also employed. Owing to the advent of wireless telegraphy it was decided by the Admiralty, in 1918, that the Naval Pigeon Service was obsolete, and the Government PIGEONS were therefore disposed of (*Referee*, 22.xii.18). At the beginning of the war the British authorities took a characteristic course in dealing with these birds. They ordered the internment, or destruction, of all PIGEONS along the coast. Thousands of lives of men depended upon the reversal of that edict, and upon the use, instead of slaughter, of the birds. The mine-sweepers were the first to realise the existence of a means of communication possible where all others failed, and an emergency Pigeon Service was established through private owners by means of which mine-sweepers were enabled to send information to shore of large minefields newly laid and other dangers of the sea (*Bird Notes and News*, vol. viii. p. 25). Gradually it was recognised that PIGEONS would prove of great military importance: steps were taken to set up an effective "carrier" service, pigeon-fanciers came forward with the utmost patriotism to present their birds, and a little later severe penalties were enforced under D.O.R.A. for shooting CARRIER PIGEONS. It was even held that it was the duty of the public, in their own interest, to feed, water, and care for any stray HOMERS which might come into their possession (*Daily Express*, 18.vii.18). In spite of these precautions, several fell victims during the shoots organised in this country to thin the immigrant hordes of WOOD PIGEONS.

Our Military Pigeon Service, under Captain A. H. Osman, grew to large proportions, and, though it was not till March 1916 that the first British PIGEONS were sent over to the Western Front, our birds soon became as useful to us as those employed by our Allies in France and Belgium, in which latter country the training and rearing of PIGEONS has long ranked as a national sport. In the earlier days old omnibuses were used as travelling lofts, but later on up-to-date motor lofts were extensively employed. The PIGEONS were taken by bicyclists in wicker crates to the front-line trenches, where they proved of the greatest use; particularly when the telegraph and telephone wires had been cut by shell fire, and when it became impossible for the intrepid "runners" to bring back messages on foot. Pigeon-post messages when written and folded are carried in a cup placed in a small cylindrical carrier of aluminium clipped to the bird's leg. The PIGEON on returning to one of the latest type of lofts, hearing its mate calling inside, finds its way to a ledge under the window fitted with hinged wires that only open inwards. Pushing through these, the bird's weight presses on the lightly balanced interior platform, completing an electric circuit and so ringing a bell, which warns the attendant in his dug-out of the arrival of a messenger. Some of the longest distances flown in the war were 300 miles, and one female PIGEON flew 166 sea-miles three weeks in succession with despatches from the North Sea. Usually the birds fly these long distances about once a week, but they require rest after them. It has been calculated that as many as 100,000 PIGEONS were employed by the British forces during the war, and their demobilisation was announced in January 1919 (*Daily News*, 22.i.19).

In November 1914 the German invaders of France issued orders by which it was "expressly forbidden to keep live PIGEONS of any breed," and a penalty of fifty francs for each bird was imposed. The wretched inhabitants reluctantly killed all the birds they could, but many escaped and were driven to the fields. Here they were shot at by any passing German soldier, and if they alighted on some peasant's roof they were driven off with volleys of stones for fear of incurring the penalty of a fine: PIGEONS had a hard time of it. It has been estimated that a million Belgian PIGEONS were stolen by the Germans during their occupation; just before the Armistice some 25,000 were taken, of which only 5,000 were found at Spandau. Little hope is entertained of recovering the remainder of the missing birds, which are believed to have been killed and eaten by the hungry German soldiers (*Daily Express*, 25.i.19).

Although on the Continent spies were arrested for making use of this medium to convey messages, no such cases appear to have been reported in this country. In this connection it is amusing to note that the recovery of birds ringed for the investigation of migration was often regarded as suspicious; a BLACK-HEADED GULL, ringed "M—VIBORG: DENMARK," which was shot in Suffolk in December 1916, was forwarded to the military authorities, who passed the ring to the Admiralty with the following comment: "This looks as if addressee had been trying to train a GULL as a carrier to England: this has often been tried, but is generally considered unreliable."

HOMING PIGEONS were extensively used by our fleet, and it is recorded that Skipper Thomas Crisp, V.C., who died at the wheel under fire from a German submarine, lived long enough to despatch a message by PIGEON: through the timely arrival of the bird his son and crew were saved. An R.A.F. seaplane, patrolling over the North Sea, made a forced descent and was in danger of being dashed to pieces by the heavy sea. The airmen released a PIGEON with a message asking for immediate help, and in twenty-two minutes the bird reached its loft twenty-two miles distant. Help was at once sent, and the airmen were found clinging to the wreckage of the machine, which was rapidly breaking up (*Daily Mail*, 30.ix.18). A touching story is told by a Canadian, Flight-Commander R. Leckie, D.S.O., in a letter home, published in an American newspaper. After an engagement with hostile aircraft over the North Sea he came down, his seaplane riddled with shrapnel, over fifty miles from land, and then had to act as rescuer and host to the crew of an aeroplane, wrecked by engine failure. Six men were thus adrift in a doomed machine, with no food and little water. The commander had four pigeons: one was released at once, a second on the next day, a third on the third day. All failed to reach home, perishing over the waste of waters. The fourth, set free in a fog, hungry and thirsty, struggled over the fifty miles of sea without a landmark and without a rest. The bird could not reach his loft, but fluttered down in a coastguard station, and there fell dead from exhaustion; but his message was delivered and six men were saved (*Bird Notes and News*, vol. viii. p. 26). A PIGEON, sent on a seaplane carrying out duties in the North Sea, brought back the message "attacked." The observer had not time to write more, and the bird itself, shot through the left eye by a bullet during the encounter which resulted in the loss of the seaplane, only just managed to struggle to its loft. It was promptly "pensioned off" war service and became the pet of the aerodrome (*Daily Chronicle*, 11.ix.18). PIGEONS once wounded while serving their country were not allowed again on duty; they were fed on the best and became perfectly tame, answering to such names as "Haig," "Kitchener," and "Amiens" (*Daily Mirror*, 20.ix.18).

HOMERS were taken up in aeroplanes and

"tossed" with messages from behind the German lines. Advantage was also taken of the fact that behind the German lines there were large towns or thickly populated areas occupied by a friendly people, many of whom, moreover, knew all about HOMING PIGEONS, as the North of France and Belgium, like Yorkshire and Lancashire, were centres of the "fancy." By a combination of close meteorological study and ingenious mechanical devices it became possible to drop baskets containing our PIGEONS on occupied areas where the chances were that they would fall into friendly hands. These hands knew where to take them, and in due course quite a large percentage arrived at our lofts bearing valuable information (*Times*, 30.xii.18). PIGEONS were also made use of for "counter-espionage." The Germans made a splendidly finished message-carrier with a red seal at the top; from time to time our troops captured German PIGEONS in the trenches, but could not use them to send messages as they had no similar holders. A medal maker of Birmingham, however, imitated the well-made German holder so perfectly that it was impossible to tell those he made from the captured original. Thereafter a number of "dud" messages were sent to German lofts with their own birds (*Daily Mail*, 9.iv.19).

In Italy, on at least one occasion, a pigeon-post message brought the news that an Austrian convoy was moving in front of the British lines; an aeroplane was at once despatched and completely disorganised the convoy (*Daily Mail*, 26.vi.18). A company of French troops, cut off from their fellows by a curtain of fire at Verdun, owed their deliverance to a HOMING PIGEON (*New York American*, 28.iv.18). One of the most important factors of the defence in the Eastern Champagne on July 15th, 1918, was the smooth working of the Information Service under the German bombardment. Each pill-box fort in the covering zone was supplied with a crate of CARRIER PIGEONS, and the birds brought back news of every movement of the enemy and every phase of the fight to the command posts. One officer commander, with experience of intelligence work, interrogated German prisoners who were brought into his pill-box as they arrived, and despatched the information derived from the bewildered Germans by "colombogram" almost as quickly as it could have been sent by telegram. In another case the garrison of a pill-box sent back by PIGEON a request that artillery should immediately open on the ground around their stronghold, taking no thought for their own safety, as the Germans were about to surround them (*Morning Post*, 19.vii.18). The officer who commanded the first Tank Corps Battalion stated that PIGEONS had frequently saved the situation for him. Neither a gas cloud nor a heavy barrage of artillery fire deterred these messengers from bringing their despatches. The battle of Monchy is alleged to have been won through a flying message to the troops at the base; a counter-attack at Arras was smashed by the same means (*Bird Notes and News*, vol. viii. p. 25).

Although the HOMING PIGEONS on the Western Front were of the greatest use, as many as a thousand birds being sometimes employed in a single engagement, their value was not always properly estimated. There is a story that, when pressed hard to find a dinner for his master, a faithful "batman" served up what he simply described as "a brace of birds." They proved excellent eating, but a subsequent enquiry from Headquarters as to the loss of two valuable HOMING PIGEONS led to investigations. The "batman" eventually revealed the origin of the dainty dish to his master, and after being warned that, if found out, it would certainly mean a court-martial, was asked if he had left any evidence, such as the basket; to which he replied, "Couldn't cook 'em without making a fire, sir" (*Daily Mail*, 3.ii.19). The men to whom the CARRIER PIGEONS were consigned occasionally became bored by their precious charges. One day a practice "PIGEON message" was received from a somewhat "fed-up" Australian battalion rather weary of sending practice PIGEON messages during many weeks. The latest message when decoded read thus:—"In view of the shortage of paper, what about crossing these birds with cockatoos and teaching them to deliver verbal messages?" (*Globe*, 31.v.18). On another occasion, during an engagement on a big scale, a certain Headquarters Staff was very anxiously awaiting news. For a long while none came. Then a PIGEON flew into sight, circled several times, and alighted on a roof. A man was sent to catch it. He brought down the packet containing the message. The Staff gathered round the officer who took the message. They listened with intense eagerness to learn the news. What the officer read out was: "I am fed up with this blasted bird" (*Daily Mail*, 14.iii.18). This story, when brought to the attention of the War Office, provoked an encomium of our Pigeon Service, which, it was said by the officer in charge, had proved invaluable, the birds frequently homing through gas clouds and barrage after all other means of communication had failed. All the birds were presented to the service from the finest strains of long-distance pedigree stock, and the majority of

Utility and Economy of Birds

the men in charge of them were life-long fanciers devoted to the work. In one of the greatest battles, where PIGEONS were largely used, 100 per cent. of the messages were delivered under most difficult circumstances, and it was stated authoritatively that thousands of lives had been saved by PIGEONS homing from seaplanes or mine-sweepers in distress (*Daily Mail*, 22.iii.18). Admiralty records showed that 95 per cent. of the several thousand PIGEONS employed in the Naval Pigeon Service came through with their messages (*Daily Mail* and *Daily Chronicle*, 7.v.18). The PIGEONS of the Royal Air Force, up till the end of 1918, had brought no fewer than 717 messages of distress from aircraft down on the surface of the water. In carrying these messages the birds covered an aggregate of 20,000 miles (*Referee*, 22.xii.18).

The Germans erected special gas-proof cotes for their PIGEONS and went so far as to camouflage their birds by giving them a coating of paint. A message taken from one of these German PIGEONS pays our troops a back-handed compliment: "Field Battery No. 36. Our telephone is out of order. Send us *at once* reinforcements. These accursed Englishmen keep us busy. Muller, 1st Lieutenant" (*Daily Mail*, 5.iv.16). By observation plus instinct most of our birds rapidly learned their route from the trenches; though shy at first, the PIGEONS got "wise" to shell fire and old birds made away from the dug-outs with knowing swiftness. PIGEONS proved hardy and recovered from exposure to gas. They were rarely shot dead while flying, and birds with shrapnel in the breast or with broken beaks gamely tried to carry their missives home. In the action which was fought in the region of the Menin Road on October 3rd, 1917, a PIGEON, No. 2,709, was despatched with a message from the front line to divisional headquarters at 1.30 p.m. During its passage it was struck by a German bullet which broke one of its legs, denuding the bone (the tibia) of all flesh, and drove the metal cylinder containing the message into the side of its body, the bullet passing out of its back. In spite

Utility and Economy of Birds

of its wounds, and although out in the wet all night, the bird struggled home to its loft, a distance of nine miles, and delivered its message at 10.53 a.m. the following day, October 4th, dying shortly after its arrival (*The Field*, 2.ii.1918). The bird has now been added to the museum of the Royal United Service Institution, Whitehall, where it may be seen stuffed in a glass case labelled "Died of wounds received in action" (*Daily Mail*, 25.vii.18). Had the feat of this PIGEON been performed by a human being, it might well have been rewarded by the V.C.

It is impossible to estimate the value of the "carrier" service to the Naval, Military, and Air Forces. Not only were our PIGEONS extensively employed on the Western Front, but also at Salonika, in Italy, Egypt, Mesopotamia, and elsewhere, and on innumerable occasions they carried life-and-death messages with superhuman pluck and perseverance. Doubtless our enemies would speak as highly of the services of their HOMERS. A German pigeon-loft with thirty-five PIGEONS, captured by the Canadians at Folies, near

Arras, on August 9th, 1918, was presented to the Zoological Society of London in October. The two Germans in charge of the loft attempted, on the near approach of the Canadians, to burn it, but our men quickly despatched the Germans and extinguished the flames. The marks of the fire, however, remain, and several bullet-holes may be seen penetrating the outside frame of the loft (*Times*, 2.xi.18).

In March 1918, when every one was invited to invest their money in War Bonds, an additional attraction was afforded by the Pigeon Post Service which carried messages from the investor's home to the Tank Bank in Trafalgar Square, notifying the amount of the investment. Queen Alexandra's PIGEON attracted a crowd of people to the mobile loft when the bird arrived, within a minute, from Marlborough House with the announcement that Her Majesty wished to purchase 500 War Savings Certificates on behalf of the Queen Alexandra League (*Globe*, 4.iii.18). In America the HOMER was likened to "the DOVE sent out from the Ark of Noah which brought wanted news then; so do the CARRIER PIGEONS of the war zone bring their messages now" (*New York American*, 28.iv.18). A recruiting message from Lady Reading was carried in May 1918 from Washington by three CARRIER PIGEONS to New York, where it was read at a mass meeting under the auspices of the British and Canadian Recruiting Committee (*The Times*, 30.v.18). In the pageant of the Lord Mayor's Show of 1918 a travelling pigeon-loft took part in the procession to remind the public of the splendid achievements performed by members of the Carrier Pigeon Service, which has been not inaptly dubbed the "First Flying Corps" (*Bird Notes and News*, vol. viii. p. 25). Before April 1919 the demobilisation of the PIGEONS and their attendants in France had taken place with the exception of birds and men selected for the Army of Occupation. Some 9,000 to 10,000 birds that had served their country well had to be disposed of. They would have been a drug on the English market if they had been sent home and the cost of the transaction would probably have been more than the birds would have realised. They were therefore sold at Courtrai, Lille, and other places in France and Belgium, and the proceeds of sale divided among charitable institutions, in accordance with the wish of the breeders who gave the birds to the country for the war (*Daily Mail*, 9.iv.19).

The HOMING PIGEON has been ridiculously libelled during the war, for no spy melodrama or novelette has been complete without one or more of these attractive birds, which are invariably represented as working for the Germans. Ever since the original war story of the market-woman of Armentières, or Arras, or Rheims (it is told by veracious eye-witnesses of all these towns and many more) whose figure attracted the attention of the alert soldiery and whose bust flew away when they arrested her, the HOMING PIGEON has laboured under a load of suspicion (*Daily Express*, 15.v.18). As a matter of fact, it may safely be said that His Majesty had no more devoted, though unwitting, servants than the HOMING PIGEONS of his army and navy.

It is of interest to note that PARROTS were employed, early in the war, at the Eiffel Tower to announce the approach of hostile aircraft. It was found at first that the birds gave warning fully twenty minutes before an aeroplane or airship could be identified by the eye or heard by the human ear. The birds, however, which could never be trained to discriminate between a French and a German aeroplane, appear to have grown indifferent or bored, so that they ceased to be trustworthy (*Daily Mail*, 1.ii.18).

It is well known that CANARIES, being about fifteen times more sensitive than a man to poisonous gases, are used in mines and in mining disasters to test atmospheric conditions and save miners or explorers from gas-poisoning. The Government Mines Committee recommended that two or three birds should be kept at rescue stations for the testing for carbon-monoxide. Our soldiers on the Western Front are said on one occasion to have been warned, by the behaviour of wild birds in the night, of a coming attack of poisonous gas. Before the smell of the fumes could be perceived in the trenches, the soldiers were awakened to their danger by the noise of birds which had detected the first fumes of the vile infection (*Bird Notes and News*, vol. vi. p. 102). CANARIES and other cage birds were extensively used by both our own and the German miners at the front, when tunnelling, to detect the presence of subterranean gas (*Daily Mail*, 29.v.18). A soldier, writing of his company's CANARY, says: "Many were the nights on which he was rudely disturbed from his slumbers, dumped unceremoniously into a sandbag, and carried through rain and snow up to the trenches. Here he would do his job underground, and as often as not reach the surface again a limp little form lying at the bottom of his cage; he never failed us, though" (*Bird Notes and News*, vol. viii. p. 26). In many cases the CANARIES, issued as tests for the presence of poisonous gas, were made pets of by our soldiers and placed by them in the safest places (*Daily Mail*, 10.iv.19).

Utility and Economy of Birds

Hundreds of "enemy" CANARIES were killed by our shell and gas but those that were rescued by our troops were, needless to say, well cared for. A demonstration of their utility was given to the members of the Congress of South-Eastern Scientific Societies on June 1st, 1918, when a bird in a cage was introduced into a chamber full of poison-gas and became unconscious before a human being, exposed to the same conditions, showed any sign of being affected (*Sunday Herald*, 2.vi.18). This war-time use of CANARIES may have been one of the reasons which caused a CANARY boom in America, where these birds are very popular. Although double the pre-war price would willingly have been paid, the birds were unprocurable; German-bred birds being out of the market, and the majority of the Norwich fanciers having joined the colours, the demand proved far greater than the supply (*Daily Mail*, 8.v.16).

It is horrible to think of CANARIES being stifled by poison-gas, and the following verses "To a CANARY in a Trench" may here be quoted:

Birds as Messengers

Bon jour, merry bird !
Your bonny life we ask,
   That we may know
   When gases blow,
And spring to don a mask.
We would that we might mask you too,
  So beautiful, so fair.
    You sing to-day
    Your roundelay,
And love is everywhere !

Bon soir, merry bird !
In war you've played your part—
   Nor knew that death
   Was in the breath
That stilled your little heart.
Your perch swings idly in your cage—
  Unscathed we march along.
    So may we learn,
    If fortune turn,
To greet death with a song !

           (*Life*: 14. xi. 18, p. 700).

It is consoling to learn that CANARIES were also used in ambulance trains to cheer our wounded soldiers with their sweet song (*Sporting and Dramatic News*, 8.vi.18).

SEA-GULLS on more than one occasion betrayed the presence of submarines and floating mines to anxious mariners. A French writer, M. Louis Rousseau, claimed them as "one of our most precious auxiliaries, who had at all times indicated to our fishermen the presence of shoals of fish, and who, when our boats and their crews were mobilised and fished for mines and submarines, imitated them and continued their service of intelligence" (*Bulletin de la S.F.P.O.*, Juin 1918). A pilot reported that while in the Channel on January 5th, 1918, he noticed some SEA-GULLS sitting upon a floating object. Upon closer investigation he saw it was a mine with five prongs. On top of each prong was perched a SEA-GULL. He just had time to alter the ship's course slightly and thus averted disaster (*Observer*, 6.1.18). A somewhat similar story is told by an officer on board a ship in the North Sea: "While watching a PUFFIN through my glasses, I suddenly saw the periscope of a German submarine appear above the water close to the bird. We altered our course just in time to evade, by a few feet, two torpedoes which were fired at us. We tried to ram the submarine, but unfortunately she dived too quickly" (*Ibis*, 1917, p. 34). The fact that SEA-GULLS were attracted by the periscope of an enemy submarine aroused the ingenuity of no less a savant than "Samuel Pepys, Junr.," who suggested that "it be ordered in the fleet that all SEA-GULLS around our ships be fed daily with herrings from an underwater boat ; so whenever they shall observe any such boat, they shall assuredly flock over it for herrings, and so its presence be made known, being that these birds can see to a great depth below the water and so keen of sight as to discern a sprat five fathoms below the surface" (*Truth*, 25.ii.1915).

The suggestion, made by *Punch*, that PARROTS should be used for propaganda work both in this country and in Germany, the propagandists abroad to be crossed with British HOMING PIGEONS (*Punch*, 27.iii.18), only aimed at the humorous. A scheme was, however, sent in all seriousness to the War Inventions Board by a man who had noticed that birds peck mortar. He suggested that a flock of CORMORANTS should be trained to feed by putting their food in lines against a wall, so that they might associate these lines with their food; they should then be taken to Essen, where they would attack the chimneys at Krupp's works with such vigour as to destroy them (*Daily Mail*, 13.i.16).

2—BIRDS AS CROP PROTECTORS

IT is the considered opinion of the greatest modern ornithologists that insectivorous birds are man's best friends, since they have been proved to be protectors of his crops. But, with the crying need for the maximum production of food, an outcry against birds in general was only to be expected. Would that the detractors of the birds' characters had been silenced for ever! But though this pious wish is far from being fulfilled, it is satisfactory to be able to record that, as the War continued, the inimical attitude of the agriculturist towards birds showed signs of abatement. Economic ornithology has not yet been sufficiently studied in Great Britain, but the laborious work of such investigators as Messrs. W. E. Collinge, C. F. Archibald, J. Gilmour, F. V. Theobald, H. S. Leigh, R. T. Gunther, and Miss Laura Florence all goes to prove the valuable assistance rendered by birds to forestry and agriculture, to say nothing of the dietetic value of Game-birds and Wildfowl. That the farmers and their "expert advisers" were, however, slow to regard the birds as the protectors of their crops, the following notes will show.

One of the features of the War was the breaking-up of thousands of acres of pasture land. This innovation revealed the presence of a corresponding amount of insect pests such as wire-worms; yet, oblivious of the fact that insect plagues can be dealt with effectually only by birds, their indiscriminate destruction was recommended by the "expert advisers" of the Board of Agriculture. In view of the fact that insectivorous birds may also eat grain, these wiseacres issued a ban against all birds, regardless of the acknowledged fact that, though birds may take a proportion of fruit or grain at harvest time, they more than justify their existence by the quantity of injurious insects they consume at other seasons of the year. Any thoughtful mind must be impressed by the wisdom of our Wild Birds Protection Acts, which protect all birds during the breeding season, a period throughout which the young of even such a harmful species as the House Sparrow is insectivorous. It must surely be the height of folly to kill birds at the very time when they are doing good, though it is arguable that it should be legal to kill a bird which is caught in the act of doing harm. No insect eater should be the object of a crusade merely because for a week or two he takes toll of the fruit. It is not just, and, more than that, it is bad policy. The attitude of him who would kill a bird for taking sixpennyworth of fruit after saving pounds' worth of produce from the insects is obviously ridiculous (*Sheffield Daily Telegraph*, 3.vii.18).

The schoolboy who translated the old adage *Medio tutissimus ibis* by *In the midst of them was the Ibis, jolly safe!* was certainly not scholarly, but his translation would be apt were it not for the avariciousness of the collector of rare British birds; to my mind our Wild Birds Protection Acts carry out its sound principle both from the bird-lover's and from the farmer's point of view. So far from authorising the destruction of birds in wartime, the authorities should have given them the benefit of extra protection. Thousands of acres of common and other open land, where LARKS and many other insectivorous birds were wont to live, were turned into camps and parade-grounds only to be trodden down by men and horses. Thousands of acres of wood and coppice were felled throughout the country in the attempt to meet the demand for timber. These results of the war have had a far-reaching effect on our bird population. A French ornithologist has stated that France, when the Germans have ceased to harry the land, will have pressing need of all her bird-life to fight the insect invaders and ravagers of her fields; in our own country the need is the same, though less tragically important (*Bird Notes and News*, vol. vi. p. 92).

Perhaps the greatest outburst against birds in general was early in 1917, when it was urged that "shoot the birds" should be the clarion cry (*Daily Mail*, 4.i.17). The formation of "SPARROW CLUBS" throughout the country was recommended, and raids against the BULLFINCH, HAWFINCH, JAY, BLACKBIRD, THRUSH, and STARLING were widely advocated. As a set-off to the Wild Birds Protection Act it was suggested that there should be a "Tame Humans Preservation Act" (*Daily Mail*, 10.i.17). To this outcry against all birds Sir Herbert Maxwell published a well-reasoned answer, drawing attention to the number of destructive insects consumed by birds, and pointing out that the indiscriminate destruction of small birds would result in as much harm as good (*Times*, 31.i.17). The SEA-GULL was accused not only of taking trout but also of taking valuable manure in collaboration with the ROOK (*Glasgow Herald*, 15.iii.17); and it was announced in May 1917 that soldiers training in England were to go on official birds-nesting expeditions, and that "as the season is well advanced troops are to go birds-nesting at once" (*Daily Mail*, 26.v.17). The Board of Agriculture, besides acquiescing in this persecution of birds, advised War Agricultural Committees to destroy ROOKERIES, extended the time for burning gorse and heather, and, finally, by reading into the law what was obviously never intended to be there, and by stretching language beyond its natural meaning, proclaimed that SPARROWS were "vermin" and might therefore be destroyed by poison on the land, in contravention of the Protection of Animals Act (*Royal Society for the Protection of Birds: Annual Report*, 1918).

I have been careful to quote from my book of newspaper cuttings chronologically, and it is therefore remarkable to find that the next entry reads: "Crops eaten by Caterpillars—A seven-mile front—A devastating plague of caterpillars reported from the Peak district of Derbyshire" (*Daily Mail*, 13.v.17). Three days later the newspapers announced: "The Caterpillars' new push—Stripping the Westmorland fells" (*Daily Mail*, 16.vi.17). Inspectors of the Board of Agriculture, investigating the cause of the plague, attributed this extraordinary abundance of the caterpillars of the Antler-moth mainly to the reduced burning of grouse moors and upland pastures, and also to the absence of PLOVERS and STARLINGS (*Dumfries and Galloway Standard*, 20.vi.17, and *Royal Society for the Protection of Birds: Annual Report*, 1918). A similar plague of caterpillars spoilt the early promise of a great fruit crop in France (*Daily Mail*, 22.vi.17).

There can be no doubt that popular feeling was against birds in general; moreover throughout 1917 there was a lamentable scarcity of the smaller species, due mainly to the abnormally severe weather conditions experienced in the earlier months of the year. This scarcity was deplored by the bird-lover, but should also have been regretted by the agriculturist, who should have realised that insects, which it is all but impossible to keep in check by human means, are effectually controlled in their earlier stages by birds.

The misdeeds of birds are much more manifest than the benefits they confer upon us, and, sure enough, with the approach of spring in 1918, the old outcry against them was reiterated in the newspapers. It was asked,

"Will some one recommend a reliable SPARROW trap, and so become a public benefactor?" (*Daily Mail*, 7.iii.18), and war against STARLINGS and BULLFINCHES and the institution of SPARROW CLUBS were again demanded. These extravagant outbursts seem, however, to have given way to saner counsels to the effect that any relaxation of the law restraining the killing of insect-eating birds would inevitably result in diminished grain, vegetable, and fruit crops, and the birds finally recommended to be kept in check, but not entirely exterminated, were SPARROWS and WOODPIGEONS (*Daily Mail*, 4.iii.18). A plague of caterpillars was prophesied early in the year, and the indiscriminate slaughter of small birds and the taking of their eggs was therefore deprecated, especially as the severe winter of 1916–17 had almost destroyed the smaller insect-eating birds by the continuous frost and snow (*Times*, 21.iii.18). An admirable letter, entitled "Plea for Protection," signed by fourteen representative ornithologists, appeared in *The Times* of April 24th, 1918, pointing out that the great majority of wild birds are beneficial to man, that the insect-eating and vermin-eating species in particular are invaluable to him in field and garden, and that the destruction of birds and eggs, even of those species deemed to be injurious, should not be permitted, since useful ones inevitably suffered also (*Times*, 24.iv.18). In April 1918 came the startling news that large numbers of MAGPIES, believed to have been driven across the Channel by the fighting in France, had invaded Romney Marsh in Kent and were attacking and killing breeding ewes (*Globe*, 10.iv.18)—a statement, I venture to think, which must be taken *cum grano salis*.

In June 1918 the prophecy as to caterpillars, made earlier in the year, was fulfilled. The plague was widespread, but was particularly severe in the south and east of England and in Derbyshire and Westmorland, where the caterpillars of the Antler-moth were rampant. Even houses were said to be invaded, and it was suggested that " POULTRY should be turned loose in quantities to consume this valuable food." In his hour of agony one sufferer wrote: "We do not want to see in this country devastated districts, such as one sees abroad, through the caterpillars being allowed to go unchecked and through the destruction of birds for sport and profit" (*Daily Mail*, 11–16.vi.18). Though regretting the means, I cannot but rejoice at the end which brought these sinners, who would not recognise the utility of birds, to repentance.

I have purposely omitted the consideration of the status of the WOOD-PIGEON, a bird which may very properly be regarded as most mischievous in respect to agriculture, but which, I must here state in common fairness, was reported as taking toll of the caterpillars in June 1918. Its food-value is certainly considerable and might almost have entitled it to have been considered in the following section, but, notwithstanding the little good it may do, it undoubtedly costs more in the damage it does when alive than it realises when killed and put on the market. During the period under review battues were organised in several counties and large numbers were shot, but it must always be remembered that these battues only take a toll of the immigrants who come to this country in autumn from the Continent, and that the definite extermination of the WOOD-PIGEON as a British bird is therefore a matter entirely out of our control.

There is no doubt that, throughout the War, the energy of the Royal Society for the Protection of Birds did much to prevent the ruthless and senseless extermination in this country of our feathered friends, who deserve their name not from a feeling of sentiment but from a grateful sense of their utility. Not only did the Society carry on a vigorous campaign in the columns of the newspapers, but it also issued a pamphlet setting out the provisions of our Wild Birds Protection Acts, printed in English, French, and Flemish, for the guidance of the numerous Belgian refugees in this country, who, it was thought, might be expected to kill birds for the pot (*Bird Notes and News*, vol. vi. p. 78). The Society also circulated from time to time carefully prepared leaflets pointing out the economic value to agriculture of bird-life, of which *Birds, Insects, and Crops*, issued in March 1917, may be noticed as but one example.

Mention may also be made of the treaty, the first instrument of its kind, made between the United States and Canada in 1917, although its conclusion was due not to the War but to the enlightened view of birds prevailing across the Atlantic. This treaty protected more than a thousand valuable species of birds from the Gulf of Mexico to the North Pole. It also provided that any bird important to agriculture as a destroyer of insects should not be killed at any time. This, it was reckoned, would save American farmers millions of dollars lost through the crop depredations of insects (*Globe*, 12.iii.18). Dr. Gordon Hewitt, referring to this treaty, gave it as his opinion that "the protection of insectivorous birds is at all times a necessary measure in crop production. At the present time, when the production of food crops is not only a national but a world necessity, the protection of such birds should be regarded as a measure of national defence"

(*Conservation of Wild Life in Canada*, 1917). A handsome bird-fountain was dedicated in the Los Angeles public park to "the little warriors of the air who are fighting for us, ... who are protecting our wheat-crops for the boys in France, who are guarding the cotton crop which is used for surgical purposes and for gun-wads, who save our forests from which we build our great ships and airplanes. The birds have been officially recognised by the United States Government for their valuable aid to horticulture and agriculture. This fountain is placed here as our personal recognition of their value" (*Bird Notes and News*, vol. viii. 1918, p. 19).

3—BIRDS AS FOOD

THE majority of edible birds, being both insectivorous and graminivorous, are both beneficial and harmful to agriculture, and are thus rather difficult to discuss from the utilitarian point of view. Personally I am of the opinion that, setting aside their important value as human food, the edible birds of Great Britain are either harmless, or do more good to the farmer than harm. I have, however, discussed the question of the utility of birds in the preceding chapter, and I do not propose to fight the battles here of the various species which have been the subjects of attack from time to time; I will simply record, more or less chronologically, the enactments which affected those birds which may be regarded as forming part of our regular food-supply.

In Germany the question of the value of GAME as food was immediately realised, and in January 1915 the Imperial authorities decreed a prolongation of the open season for PHEASANTS. Ordinarily the season closed on February 1st; the new regulation extended the date to March 1st. The same decree abolished, for the duration of the War, certain restrictions on the sale and shipment of GAME shot in the province of Hanover, which abounds in well-stocked preserves, including several of the Kaiser's favourite shooting-boxes (*Daily Mail*, 11.i.15). The Grand Duke of Mecklenburg-Strelitz gave orders that GAME in his forests was no longer to be exported but that it was to be reserved exclusively for sale within the Duchy or given to hospitals, and orders were issued to shoot more GAME than usual (*Kölnische Zeitung*, 8.x.15). In May 1916 the German Government ordered CROWS, SPARROWS, STARLINGS, STORKS and ROOKS to be killed for food (*Westminster Gazette*, 13.v.16), and the retail price of a ROOK at this period is alleged to have varied from 1s. to 1s. 6d. (*Daily Mail*, 19.vii.17).

As regards Great Britain: a Bill was

introduced into Parliament in 1915 to allow of GROUSE being shot on August 5th instead of the 12th, but, after being passed by the House of Lords, it was thrown out by the Commons amid cries of "We want to shoot Germans, not GROUSE." The season 1915–16 proved exceptionally good for GROUSE. At Abbeystead, in Lancashire, the record bag of 2,929 was obtained by eight guns on August 12th, and reports from all parts of the country testified to the superabundance of GROUSE. But so great was the difficulty in getting drivers, and even guns to shoot, that I know of one celebrated Yorkshire moor, usually let for £4,000 per annum, for which but £100 was offered, and the would-be tenant afterwards heard that had he offered £150 he would probably have got it. In Westmorland over one hundred boy scouts were employed as GROUSE drivers in August 1915. The prices for GAME in Leadenhall Market were nothing unusual. In November 1915 it was asked, in the House of Commons, whether, in view of the reduction in the amount of cereals to be raised in the United

Kingdom next year, it would be thought advisable to levy a tax of 5s. per head on all hand-reared PHEASANTS, or, alternatively, £100 upon every person preserving BIRDS or buying eggs for this purpose (*Pall Mall Gazette*, 16.xi.15).

Maintaining the chronological arrangement of my notes, I have next to note that in March 1916 it was stated that many dozens of BLACKBIRDS, THRUSHES, MISSEL-THRUSHES, LARKS, and REDWINGS, alleged to have come from Norfolk, Lincolnshire, and other parts of England, were being exposed for sale as food in one of the West-end shops of London (*Times*, 31.iii.16). The trivial proposition that small birds, the guardians of our crops, should themselves be utilised as "food for the people" could only have been made by the blundering of ignorance. The following ironic reproach is so neat that it merits repetition:

> I saw with open eyes
> Singing-birds sweet
> Sold in the shops
> For the people to eat:
> Sold in the shops of
> Stupidity Street.

Utility and Economy of Birds

> I saw in a vision
> The worm in the wheat,
> And in the shops nothing
> For the people to eat:
> Nothing for sale in
> Stupidity Street.

(*Royal Society for the Protection of Birds: Annual Report*, 1918.) A question, asked in the House of Commons, elicited the reply from the Home Secretary that the Metropolitan Police found no reason to think that, except in rare cases, SONG-BIRDS were being sold for food in contravention of the law; suitable action had been taken, and he sincerely trusted that the barbarous practice of killing SONG-BIRDS for food would not take root in this country (*Hansard, H. of C.* vol. 81, No. 32, Wed. 19.iv.16).

In June 1916 there was published in a daily newspaper the portrait of "the first woman gamekeeper" (*Daily Mail*, 1.vi.16); but as the War went on women took over more and more men's work, and even "lady rabbit catchers" became quite fashionable. The absence of men led to much less shooting both of birds and of beasts, and not a few deer forests, which formerly had been sheep ground but had been given up to deer when "stalking" was at its height, now reverted to their original state. Great Britain at war commended itself as a background to an American short-story writer, who wrote in 1916: "A GOLDEN PHEASANT came calmly by, for this year the twelfth of August signified a far different shooting and the coverts were undisturbed" (*Globe*, 4.viii.16).

It was only to be expected that WILD-FOWLING by professional puntsmen and others should have been much out of favour with the naval authorities on the east coast, and restrictions, almost prohibitive in their severity, were issued under the Defence of the Realm Regulations (*Daily Mail*, 10.ix.16). As a result, WATERFOWL became much tamer; but although they seemed to realise that aeroplanes, patrol boats, gunfire, etc., were harmless to them, they still seemed to recognise a gunning punt as hostile (*Field*, 30.iii.18, p. 447). Another effect of the Admiralty's restrictions was observed off East Lothian, where some islands, on which for many years a pair of PEREGRINES had tried to breed, were put out of bounds, to the advantage of the PEREGRINES, which are believed to have nested, and also of a small colony of ROCK-DOVES, which before had been annually threatened with extinction (*Country Life*, 2.ix.16). Towards the end of 1916 suggestions appeared in the newspapers that, as there were no shooting parties, soldiers should enter upon preserves and estates and kill a proper amount of GAME, paying the owners a fair price per head for the GAME shot; it was further suggested that the GAME would be very useful for food and that the shooting would be most excellent practice for the New Armies (*Daily Mail*, 18.xi.16). Other letters appeared about this time suggesting all sorts of birds as valuable additions to our menu, young CORMORANTS, HERRING-GULLS, and GANNETS, especially the last, being recommended (*Daily Mail*, 19.ii.17). These letters were devoured with avidity by our enemies, and the Berlin *Zeitung am Mittag*, quoting the "London newspapers," literally "gulled" its readers into the belief that we were starving: "The English may print as many braggart statistics as they choose about the failure of the German U-boats, but a glance at the English newspapers reveals a far different situation, for in their editorial columns the prevailing terror of starvation is palpably evident. Unrest, discontent, and anxiety are making themselves felt more acutely day by day, and already the most unlikely articles are being seized on with avidity for food. In London they are now eating smoked SEA-GULLS, not only the home product, but also great quantities that are being imported from New Zealand ready cured. Loud and bitter are the complaints about the greasy flavour of these birds, but the newspapers are rising to the occasion and filling column on column with the most impossible recipes to show the wretched islanders that SEA-GULL may be made as tasty as TURKEY OR GOOSE" (*Daily Express*, 28.iii.17).

Early in 1917 orders were issued forbidding the rearing of PHEASANTS and the feeding of GAME on any grains or any other products required for food or feeding stuffs;

owners of PHEASANTS were expected to kill off their birds as far as possible before the end of the season, so that they might not live to feed on the growing grain of the following harvest (*Daily Mail*, 12.i.17). In spite of these restrictions it is remarkable that, some months later, not a few persons were prosecuted for feeding hand-reared PHEASANTS on corn (*Globe*, 4.v.17). On February 13th, 1917, it was stated officially in Parliament that it had been decided that occupiers of agricultural land should have a concurrent right of killing PHEASANTS on the same lines that they had in respect of ground game, without any limitation as regards a close time for breeding (*Daily Mail*, 14.ii.17). Thereupon ensued a literary warfare in the newspapers as to whether the PHEASANT was more useful to the farmer as an insect killer than harmful as a grain eater. On February 23rd and March 13th and 30th were issued orders, known as "The Destruction of PHEASANTS Orders," under the Defence of the Realm Regulations, that the Board of Agriculture might (with a view to preventing or reducing injury to crops, trees, or pasturage by GAME, hares, or rabbits, or to secure for the food-supply of the country any migratory or wild bird) depute any body to take such action as might be necessary, provide for the disposing of birds, hares, or rabbits thus killed, and authorise the killing and selling of GAME at any time which might otherwise be illegal. Any one authorised to kill or dispose of GAME was exempted from having a game licence, but was granted no exemption from the Gun Licence Act. The season for killing PHEASANTS, but for no other GAME, was extended to March 31st in England and Wales, and for selling up to April 15th.

With a view to increasing food production, an Order in Council was made on March 30th, 1917, legalising any occupier of land in Scotland to "make muirburn," with certain restrictions as to damage, at any time between October 1st and April 30th. This order might more reasonably have been restricted to March 31st, so as not to interfere with the GROUSE when nesting, for, after all, the GROUSE is a valuable bird. The Commission which investigated GROUSE disease, in 1905–11, estimated that the gross rental of GROUSE moors in England and Scotland amounted to no less than £1,270,000 annually. It must here be noticed that the proposal to allow of GROUSE being shot on August 5th, which had been so ignominiously turned down in the House of Commons in 1915, was now effected, as regards England and Wales, by an enactment, under the Defence of the Realm Regulations, authorising the killing of GROUSE on August 6th. It may also be observed that GROUSE disease, probably due to overstocking in 1915–16 and 1916–17, was rampant on many moors, particularly in Scotland. At least one County Executive Committee in Scotland availed itself of the powers conferred on it in connection with food production, by taking possession of a large GROUSE moor and appointing the tenant on the estate as their agent to secure the efficient grazing of the moor by sheep (*Daily Mail*, 18.vi.17). Feeling ran high in Scotland that the PHEASANT should not receive the same treatment as across the Border,

Birds as Food

and it was urged that agricultural tenants should have the right to kill PHEASANTS destroying crops, and that this right should be extended to include GROUSE and BLACK-GAME (*Dumfries and Galloway Standard*, 13.ii.18).

During the season 1917–18 the shortage of materials with which to make sporting ammunition proved a real drawback to shooting for the pot, and it was even suggested that owners of shootings, as a consequence, should be remitted the rates they paid on the sporting value of their properties (*Daily Mail*, 10.viii.17). Cartridges, which before the war were sold for 8*s*. 4*d*. per 100, found eager buyers, when indeed they could be got, at 20*s*. to 25*s*. per 100. The season proved a most prolific one for wild PHEASANTS, and large bags were made throughout the country. It was remarked that although these wild birds did not fly so uniformly high, they flew far more cunningly, and were much more wary, than the hand-reared birds of peacetime. About Christmas, when the price of all game and poultry was at a premium,

PHEASANTS were fetching as high as a guinea apiece in the retail shops.

In March 1918 the Board of Agriculture for Scotland authorised WILD GEESE to be killed and sold up to the 31st of the month in many counties : by no means a bad war measure, but one which would hardly find favour with the bird-lover in time of peace (*Dumfries and Galloway Standard*, 9.iii.18). On March 27th, 1918, the Ministry of Food outlined a scheme for obtaining as large a supply as possible of GAME, WILDFOWL, and rabbits during the ensuing season (*Globe*, 27.iii.18). Under the rationing restrictions, rules were laid down as regards the amount of GAME or POULTRY which might be eaten. Special concessions were, in April 1918, made to those persons, including their families and dependents, who reared POULTRY. In the case of GAME, the host, also his gamekeepers and guests, were entitled to take the GAME at a reduced rate of coupons (*Daily Mail*, 11.iv.18). As the result of a conference with the salesmen at Smithfield and Leadenhall Markets, the Food Controller, in

Birds as Food

May, fixed the prices of GAME and POULTRY as follows: old HENS and young CHICKENS, 2s. 4d. per lb.; old and young TURKEYS, 2s. 2d.; GOSLINGS and GEESE, 1s. 4d.; DUCKLINGS and DUCKS, 1s. 6d.; cock PHEASANTS, 5s. 8d. each; hen PHEASANTS, 5s. 2d.; old PARTRIDGES, 1s. 9d., young, 3s. 6d.; old GROUSE, 2s. 6d., young, 5s. (*The Times*, 25.v.18). The Ministry of Food, in July, issued regulations regarding the disposal of GAME. The owner, or occupier, of a shooting was held responsible for detaching the appropriate number of coupons from his food card, as a "self-supplier," for GAME consumed by his household, and it was made incumbent on any purchaser or recipient of GAME to do the same, but under a different category, as a receiver of "direct supplies." The scale established for a "self-supplier" was: PHEASANT, WILD DUCK, GUINEA-FOWL, CAPERCAILZIE, one coupon for each two birds; GROUSE, PARTRIDGE, BLACKGAME, WIGEON, one coupon for each four birds; TEAL, PTARMIGAN, WOODCOCK, one coupon for each eight birds; PLOVER, one coupon for each twelve birds; and QUAIL and SNIPE, one coupon for each sixteen birds. The scale for those in receipt of "direct supplies" was halved: thus, PHEASANT, WILD DUCK, etc., one coupon for each bird; PLOVER, one coupon for each six birds, and so on (*The Field*, 3.viii.18, p. 103).

The inclusion of GUINEA-FOWL among GAME BIRDS provoked humorous queries as to where the best shooting might be obtained, on what date the shooting opened, and whether it was legitimate to shoot them on the ground. It was even suggested that the Ministry of Food had been rearing GUINEA-FOWL with a view to increasing the food-supply of the country (*The Times*, 8.viii.18). Shortly afterwards a ludicrous statement appeared in print that WILD DUCK, PLOVER, SNIPE, and WATER-HENS were being bred at the Edmonton District Council's sewage farm (*Evening News*, 19.viii.18).

In July 1918 the Board of Agriculture authorised the killing of GROUSE and BLACK-GAME in England and Wales as from August 6th, and the Board of Agriculture of

Scotland made similar provision for that country. In Ireland, however, August 12th was still adhered to as the opening day for GROUSE shooting. On July 22nd a deputation from the National Farmers' Union of Scotland was received by the Board of Agriculture in Edinburgh on the subject of damage done to crops by winged GAME, and, in view of the approaching harvest, it was promised that the matter should receive immediate attention (*Dumfries and Galloway Standard*, 24.vii.18). It may be noted that in America the protection of the upland game-birds was discussed, in New York in 1918, at the fourth National Conference of the Game Protection Association. A shorter open season and the provision of sanctuaries were the outcome of the discussion, which was prompted by the desire to increase the food-supply (*New York Times*, April 1918). Although this cannot be regarded entirely as a war measure, it is another demonstration of the systematic manner in which the economic value of birds is considered by our American allies: *Utinam sic omnes.*

Utility and Economy of Birds

The difficulty, experienced in this country in the previous season, of obtaining sporting ammunition was minimised by cartridge dealers being allowed to sell not more than 500 cartridges a fortnight to holders of game-licences, or 300 cartridges a fortnight to holders of gun-licences, on the production of their licences, the price of cartridges being fixed at a maximum of 20s. per 100. Many a grouse-moor went a-begging: the shooting of 900 GROUSE in Peeblesshire was offered at £100, 600 and 500 GROUSE in Argyllshire were advertised at £100 and £60 respectively, and the celebrated Bowes Moor, of 12,000 acres, once more reverted to being shot over by "ticket-holders" limited in number to twenty-four (*The Field*, 10.viii.18). GAME throughout the country proved to be plentiful on the whole, though GROUSE and BLACK-GAME were below the average; PHEASANTS were as numerous as in the preceding season, and PARTRIDGES were in many places more than usually abundant. The legal period for shooting GROUSE and BLACK-GAME was extended, as in 1918, to January 20th, 1919.

Birds as Food

One of the first indications of the desire to return to the regimen of pre-war days was the revocation, in February 1919, of the PHEASANTS (Rearing) Order, and the Feeding of Game Order of 1917 (*Morning Post*, 1.ii.19), so that once more the feeding of game-birds with cereals, and the hatching and rearing of PHEASANTS, became legal.

4—BIRDS' EGGS AS FOOD

BACON and eggs were, before the War, a time-honoured dish in many a British home, but, with the advent of compulsory rationing for man, beast, and FOWL, both became comparatively scarce visitors to our breakfast-table. The amount of bacon per head was scrupulously cut down, and the difficulty in obtaining food for FOWLS made eggs most expensive to procure. It is recognised by medical men that eggs are not a luxury for wounded soldiers, but an item of diet, always important and in gas cases essential. Egg collections for the wounded were made from time to time throughout the country, a notable effort being that of May 27th, 1918, when it was stated that the National Egg Collection had then distributed over 30,000,000 eggs to wounded soldiers and sailors, and required 1,000,000 every week to meet all demands. In January 1919 it was announced that 41,000,000 eggs, of a total capital value of £430,619, had been distributed to base hospitals in France and at home (*Field*, 25.i.19).

In March 1917 the value of GULLS' eggs as food was bruited about, and several questions on the subject were asked in the House of Commons. The attendant dangers of taking the eggs of those species which nest on cliffs proved insurmountable, and possibly the difficulty of collection of the eggs of the BLACK-HEADED GULL made this scheme impracticable. Nevertheless the Home Office, acting under the advice of the Board of Agriculture, issued special orders removing protection, in certain counties, until June 21st from the eggs of the GUILLEMOT, RAZORBILL, PUFFIN, BLACK-HEADED GULL, and other GULLS. The main difficulty in connection with the taking the eggs of GULLS and other sea-fowl was the impossibility of guaranteeing that they were fresh; for it was realised that if incubated, even in the slightest degree, the egg would be unsaleable.

The relatively smaller numbers and more

scattered nesting-places of such species as COOTS, MOORHENS, MALLARD, and even scarce DUCKS prohibited any idea of taking their eggs on anything like a commercial basis. We were told that PHEASANTS' eggs were eaten by the Royal Family, while at Windsor in 1916, instead of PLOVERS' eggs (*Daily Mail*, 8.v.16), and these latter, being regarded as absolute luxuries, found but few buyers in the shops at 8*d.* instead of the pre-war 2*s.* 6*d.* apiece.

Early in 1918 the newspapers again resounded the cry, urging the collection of SEAGULLS', GUILLEMOTS', and PUFFINS' eggs (*Daily Mail*, 25.i.18). On February 22nd the Board of Agriculture for Scotland issued a circular suggesting the taking of the eggs of the BLACK-BACKED, LESSER BLACK-BACKED, HERRING, and COMMON GULLS for food, but advised that the BLACK-HEADED GULL, in view of its predominating insectivorous diet, should not be molested. Within six weeks, however, the restriction regarding the collection of the eggs of the last-named species was removed. In May 1918

GULLS' eggs, priced "Only 6d. each," were on sale in London shops; but as ordinary HENS' eggs were offered at 4d. each at the time it would appear that the supply must have been so small that they were regarded as luxuries.

A point which seems to have escaped the notice of those who advised the taking of the eggs of game-birds and wild-fowl is that the food-value of the egg, if left unmolested to be hatched and reared to maturity, would, in some sixteen weeks' time, be greatly in excess of the food-value of the egg itself.

In September 1918 the Ministry of Food, in order that the ordinary channels of distribution of FOWLS' eggs should not be interfered with beyond ensuring that big towns in industrial districts should have their fair proportion, instituted three grades of eggs: (1) Eggs other than imported and preserved eggs weighing over 1½ oz.; (2) imported and preserved eggs over 1½ oz.; (3) all eggs less than that weight. Thus a clean sweep was made of the traditional trade classification, which recognised "ninety-nine different varieties of eggs ranging from new-laid to fresh Egyptian, pudding, etc." (*The Globe*, 12.ix.18). A little later the Ministry began to distribute the large stocks of imported and pickled eggs which it had acquired, and fixed the shop price at 4½d. each. A new "Order" announced that in the event of a shortage of eggs priority in distribution would be given to hospitals, and stated that the expression "eggs" meant eggs laid by any bird (*Daily Mail*, 21.ix.18).

II—SUFFERINGS OF BIRDS IN THE WAR

5—EFFECT OF THE WAR ON BIRDS IN CAPTIVITY, AND DURING SEVERE WEATHER

BIRDS in captivity became more and more difficult to keep as the supply of cereals, bananas, eggs, bread, etc., were restricted as the War went on. Never, for example, were so many PARROTS freely offered on loan to the Zoological Society of London, and never were the offers so systematically refused. Incidentally may I say that it was even more difficult to maintain the animals, and the more common varieties were reluctantly put down. The week before the rationing system came into force in London, on February 24th, 1918, the Society's bull bison was killed and was apportioned out to the garden's staff. In all the zoological gardens in Germany and Austria the animals were reported to have been killed early in 1916 to save the cost of their upkeep, and even those in the famous Tiergarten in Berlin and the magnificent menagerie at Schönbrunn were sacrificed. It must, however, be noted that in May 1918 the Berlin Zoological Gardens Association was sued for 10,000 marks damages by a landlord whose block of flats adjoined the Zoo. He claimed that the menagerie—including both the caged animals and the Berliners who made too much noise while eating on the fashionable Zoo dining-terrace—so disturbed the peace of the neighbourhood that tenants for his flats could only be secured with difficulty (*Daily Mail*, 17.v.18).

In the battle-areas pet birds ran no less risks than their owners. Among the tragedies of the War must be included the destruction of the incomparable collection of live birds at Villers-Bretonnaux, belonging to Lieutenant J. Delacour, which occurred during the German push towards Amiens in the earlier part of 1918. The collection comprised some 360 birds, representing 141 species, all of which were destroyed (*Avicultural Magazine*, vol. ix. pp. 269, 305).

Effect of Captivity and Severe Weather

The interruption in the fishing industry seriously affected the GULLS, which depend so much on the refuse thrown overboard by the fishermen. They became ravenous, and it was reported that late in January 1915, when the German cruiser *Blücher* was sunk in the North Sea, enormous flocks of GULLS were attracted by the dead fish killed by the explosions incident to the sea fight (*Zoologist*, 1915, p. 97).

Wild birds, which in days of peace profited by the crumbs from the rich man's table, found that even these were cut off when an economy in bread was enforced by law. Although, in the earlier stages of the War, it was no uncommon sight to see a wounded soldier in his distinctive blue uniform feeding the GULLS, yet it became criminal, as the War dragged on, to indulge in such acts of charity. On June 9th, 1917, an elderly woman was fined £2 2s. at Woking for giving bread to wild birds; she stated that she had lost her only son in Mesopotamia, that all she used were the dirty bottom crusts she could not eat, and that she had fed the birds for seventy years and would continue to do so (*Bird Notes and News*, vol. vii. p. 88). A man was fined £2 2s. at Greenwich on July 9th, 1917, for throwing out half a slice of bread for birds (*Daily Mail*, 10.vii.17), and similar prosecutions were, at this period, not uncommon. A bird hostel, where soldiers' pet birds were received and taken care of during their owner's absence, was set up at Brixton by an "old contemptible" (*Daily Mail*, 1.viii.18), who must have had a warm heart both for birds and soldiers. Early in 1919, when the food restrictions were somewhat relaxed, birds fared better, and our returning soldiers got a very warm welcome at London Bridge from the PIGEONS. The birds were so accustomed to sharing the buns provided for Tommy at Lady Limerick's buffet that they learnt the arrival times of the leave trains and gathered round to welcome with cupboard love. An eye-witness writes: "I saw one Tommy receiving kisses from three PIGEONS at the same time; one was on his shoulder, one on his head, and the third was pecking at the bun he held in his hand" (*Star*, 3.i.19).

Effect of Captivity and Severe Weather

Although the War accounted for many changes, it can hardly be accused of affecting our weather, though there are many persons who firmly believe that the intense gunfire often induced rain and caused cold winds. In south-east England the wetness was phenomenal during the War (*Globe*, 24.vii.18), and it is certainly remarkable that the meteorological conditions prevailing in Great Britain should have been so abnormal, as the following observations show: 1914—December, wettest on record. 1915—January, severe floods; August, extraordinarily frequent thunderstorms, nine within eleven days; December, very wet and stormy. 1916—January, mildest for half a century; March, severest for fifty-eight years, on 28th the greatest gale for a century; August and September, wettest for thirteen years (*Daily Mail*, 16.iv.17). The winter of 1916–17 was the coldest experienced in many places for twenty-two years, and its effect on bird-life may be summed up in the words of the Anglo-Saxon Chronicle for the year 671: "This year was the great destruction of birds."

Sufferings of Birds

Other severe winters, fatal to many birds, were those of 1408, 1838, 1855, 1860, 1878-9, 1880-1, 1890-1, and 1894-5. The first real cold was not felt till the end of November 1916, and, though January and February 1917 were abnormally cold and wintry, it was not till March and April that our resident birds, weakened by the privations of the preceding months, died wholesale of starvation. In some localities not a few species entirely disappeared, and in others many species were brought perilously near extinction. PLOVERS and WADING-BIRDS were naturally early victims, many of the former being picked up as mere skeletons, and quantities of the smaller insectivorous birds suffered likewise. Doubtless the winter of 1916-17, which it is reckoned destroyed three-fourths of the insect-eating wild birds, did much to account for the dearth of useful birds in the following early summer (*British Birds Magazine*, vol. xi. pp. 266-71, and vol. xii. pp. 26-35). June 1917 was remarkable for exceptionally severe thunderstorms, and on the 16th there occurred the worst within living memory.

Effect of Captivity and Severe Weather

August proved abnormally wet, windy, and cold, but thereafter the weather was not extraordinary, though early in July 1918 many parts of the country were threatened with drought. According to the British Rainfall Organisation, however, there was, contrary to the popular impression, no drought this summer (*Observer*, 14.vii.18). This may be so theoretically, or according to the arbitrary rules adopted by the organisation as to what constitutes a drought, but from all parts of the country complaints were rife as to the shortage of rain, and in many parish churches prayers for rain were offered up.

Birds in London, as the War dragged on, found many of their sanctuaries invaded by the presence of soldiers and even desecrated by the erection of "temporary buildings." Those of us who have had to live throughout the year in London must have been struck by the amount of bird life to be seen in the metropolis. From my dentist's chair in Harley Street I once saw a KESTREL hovering, and was assured, when gagged and bound I tried to point the bird out to him, that it was "only a momentary pang." The STARLINGS circling nightly around Nelson's Column, the THRUSHES singing daily in Belgrave Square, the MALLARD passing over St. George's Hospital every evening, were all familiar sights. The War had not, however, been long begun before many sheets of water were drained: notably the lake in St. James's Park, where, not long after, arose a group of Government buildings appropriately known as "Lake Dwellings." With the prolongation of the War came the erection of other Government and Y.M.C.A. buildings in all available spaces, including many of the London parks and squares, thus banishing former denizens, and also migratory visitors, which used to lend so much interest and beauty to them (*Westminster Gazette*, 9.iv.18).

6—DESTRUCTION OF BIRDS AT SEA

IN October 1914 were published the first reports of sea-birds, disabled by oil, having been washed ashore on the coast of South Norfolk and North Suffolk (*Zoologist*, 1915, p. 96). In 1915 similar occurrences were reported off Sussex and Kent in January; off Holy Island in January and February; off Romney Marsh on June 9th and 10th; off the Isle of May and coast of Fife on June 16th. From June 21st to July 1st numbers of sea birds and land birds were killed by a quantity of crude oil off St. Andrews, and an observer stated that the oil stuck to the birds like bird-lime and that he buried no less than 269 GUILLEMOTS (*Scottish Naturalist*, 1917, p. 78). Heavy mortality among sea birds, from a like cause, was reported in Largo Bay, from the River Tay opposite Dundee to Kirkcaldy, on June 24th; and off Kingsdown and Dungeness in November, when a KING-EIDER and hundreds of SCOTERS and GUILLEMOTS perished; in some cases the oil is said to have penetrated the skin to the flesh beneath. Doubtless the birds came inland on account of the irritating effect of the oil, and, as it floated in a thin layer on the surface of the sea, it was only when wading ashore in the more shallow water that their feet became affected (*British Birds Magazine*, vol. ix. pp. 252–3). On January 9th and 10th, 1916, sea-birds were found, killed by oil, off Dungeness (*British Birds Magazine*, vol. iv. pp. 152–3), and in January off Blackpool and Lytham (*tom. cit.* p. 256). Investigations proved that some of these dates synchronised with the sinking of British oil-ships in the North Sea, and it is to be hoped that the others indicated the sinking of German submarines or other oil-using enemy craft. In one case the sea birds were described as sitting on the rocks in a very dirty condition, stained dark brown and practically helpless, quantities being washed ashore caked with oil. The beach was covered with little patches of oil, and amongst the rocks it was much thicker, having the appearance of thick chocolate sauce, and being in some places six or seven inches deep (*Scottish Naturalist*, September 1915, pp. 282–4). The birds, with their feathers matted with oil, were unable either to fly or dive, and in the end starved to death. GUILLEMOTS, RAZORBILLS, and PUFFINS died in enormous numbers, and EIDER-DUCKS also suffered (*Bristol Times and Mirror*, 19.v.16). An observer of the November catastrophe writes that the beach was sticky and foul, and one day the breakers were black, the feathers of the GULLS were discoloured, GUILLEMOTS especially suffered and even died because of the clogging of their plumage and their consequent inability to fly; prawns were uneatable, and even fish were tainted from the same cause (*Westminster Gazette*, 8.xi.15). On one occasion a GREEN PARROT completed the list of dead, probably a pet washed off some ship (*Country Life*, 2.ix.16).

No such catastrophes were again recorded till the end of April 1918, when a number of

Sufferings of Birds

GUILLEMOTS were found on the beach near Berwick in a helpless state, their wings and plumage being covered with oil which prevented their flying or diving, and when approached they tried to walk away, but were easily captured (*Times*, 29.iv.18). It is curious that between these dates there should be an absence of similar reports; undoubtedly many oil-carrying or oil-using craft must have been sunk in 1916 and 1917, and it can hardly be supposed that the sea birds had learned to shun the death-dealing oil, and then forgot their lesson. Probably there were many unobserved bird-tragedies on the high-seas. When an American steamer was wrecked on the Goodwin Sands in February 1919, about 1,500 tons of oil escaped into the sea. So thickly did it collect on the surface that GULLS became unable to plunge in search of food. Their heads, beaks, and feathers became covered, and many were washed ashore in an exhausted condition (*Daily Mail*, 3.ii.19).

GULLS were occasionally killed by shell-fire from our ships when at gun practice at sea. The gunfire seemed to attract the GULLS in hundreds; they would therefore seem to have realised that quantities of fish would be killed by the concussion (*Bird Notes and News,* vol. vii. p. 106).

7—EFFECT OF AIR-RAIDS AND AIRCRAFT ON BIRDS

I WILL continue to confine my remarks to the effect of the War on birds as regards Great Britain. In a subsequent chapter I shall deal with observations on birds in the actual war zones, but I now propose to record how air-craft, gun-fire, air-raids, and the like affected birds, particularly in this country.

That birds should regard an aeroplane, especially one of the monoplane type, as a huge FALCON, or other RAPTOR, might be considered as not only probable but natural, and there are numerous records of birds being obviously terrified by them (*Scottish Naturalist*, 1916, pp. 39, 164). GULLS, in the early days of the War, were sadly put about and scared by aeroplanes that hovered over the Breydon flats, but they soon began to pay no heed to them (*Zoologist*, 1915, p. 95). On

Effect of Air-raids and Air-craft

some occasions the birds' curiosity seems to have been aroused rather than their fear, and a flock of BLACK-HEADED GULLS, in Perthshire, were seen to pursue three hydro-planes (*Scottish Naturalist*, 1916, p. 66). On the approach of an aeroplane after dark to a fir wood, it was noticed that the WOOD-PIGEONS, which had come in to roost, rose in a mass and fluttered noisily round and round, PHEASANTS crowed and flew to and fro, and all the small birds twittered and called. A WHITETHROAT and a WILLOW WARBLER began snatches of song and broke off abruptly; only a LONG-EARED OWL sat tight and showed no fear (*Bird Notes and News*, vol. vi. p. 103). A bird-lover who lives in Kensington Palace Green tells me that the birds were very much alarmed by the earlier raids. SPARROWS and OWLS became restless about an hour or thirty minutes beforehand. A GREEN PARROT shrieked repeatedly. On one occasion a SPARROW fainted, but, after having been kept in the house all night, flew away next morning. A tame PIGEON, which was always very nervous, sat in its owner's hand in a state of tension with legs and wings stiff. As the raids became more frequent, however, the birds seemed to become more accustomed to them, and their behaviour could no longer be depended on as a warning of approaching aircraft. JACKDAWS were observed, in a French town, to leave their homes in the steeples and throw themselves upon aeroplanes, clinging to them and attacking them with their beaks as if to drive away these gigantic and unknown birds of prey (*Bird Notes and News*, vol. vii. p. 105). The fact that PARROTS were employed, early in the war, to announce the approach of hostile aircraft to Paris, has already been recorded when dealing with birds as messengers.

A friendly rivalry in supplying aeroplanes was encouraged in our Colonies. The planters of Ceylon conceived the idea of naming their gifts after birds, thus their first three contributions were christened "PADDY-BIRD," "DEVIL-BIRD," and "NIGHTJAR" (*Daily Mail*, 11.xi.15). Some time later the Parliamentary Air Committee suggested that army aeroplanes should be designated as "land birds" and seaplanes as "sea birds" (*Daily Mail*, 17.viii.16). One type of German machine was known as "TAUBE"—surely a misnomer!

Among the many ornithological terms subsequently adopted by our Naval, Military, and Air Forces may be mentioned the W.R.E.N.S., to denote the Women's Royal Naval Service, and the PENGUINS, as a distinctive name for the women attached to the Royal Air Force, which force was known as ROOSTERS (men who could fly) and FLEDGELINGS (men who were learning). No term was, however, more apt than that of KIWI to denote the Royal Air Force staff officer whose terrestrial duties rendered him incapable of flight. These are but examples of avian nomenclature as applied to our Forces, and will suffice as typical of their ingenious adoption.

The formation of aerodromes in various parts of the country had but little effect on the bird population in their vicinity. PARTRIDGES haunted the precincts of more than one of our largest airship sheds, and, in spite

Sufferings of Birds

of the almost incessant noise associated with these establishments, the birds in general did not seem to avoid them. It was, however, recorded that two large ancient ROOKERIES, one about a quarter and the other half a mile away, were deserted in 1915 on account of a field being used habitually for the descent of aeroplanes (*Observer*, 5.ix.15).

Sound-waves of great explosions have been found to travel long distances from the centre of the disturbance. When the Silvertown munitions factory exploded in East London on January 19th, 1917, it was heard 128 miles away (*Proc. Roy. Soc. Edin.*, vol. xxxviii. p. 115), and other great explosions have been distinguished at distances varying from 90 to 186 miles (*Nature*, 1917, p. 439). A limited number of observations tend to show that throughout a large part of the area over which the sound-waves are audible, birds are affected by the disturbance. The immediate cause of their disquiet is unknown, but it is supposed to be due either to actual perception of the sound of explosions or to shock caused by air-wave concussion (*Scottish*

Naturalist, 1917, p. 140). The Zeppelin raids, a feature of the War early in 1915, were nearly always heralded in this country by the crowing of PHEASANTS, and the sensitiveness of this species to distant sounds was frequently a subject of comment. There seems no reason to suppose that PHEASANTS have keener powers of hearing than men; it appears more probable that these birds are alarmed by the sudden quivering of the trees, on which they happen to be perched, at the time of an explosion (*Proc. Roy. Soc. Edin.*, vol. xxxviii. p. 125). It was said that when PHEASANTS began to talk the airman got ready to fly and the anti-aircraft gunner turned out. The crowing of PHEASANTS often preceded by fifteen minutes to half an hour the approach of hostile aircraft (*Daily Mail*, 1.ii.18). During the first Zeppelin raid in January 1915, PHEASANTS at Thetford and Bury St. Edmunds, thirty-five to forty miles from the area over which the Zeppelins flew, shrieked themselves hoarse (*Daily Mail*, 1.ii.18). In one of the early battles in the North Sea, PHEASANTS as far west as Cumberland were recorded as having manifested an uncanny knowledge of some unusual atmospheric disturbance (*Globe*, 26.vi.16). Gamekeepers on the east coast used to say that they always knew when enemy raids had commenced, "for the PHEASANTS call us day and night" (*Globe*, 28.ix.17). On March 7th, 1918, about 10.30 p.m., PHEASANTS near Chichester crowed loudly; possibly the excitement, so to speak, passed along from the north-east of Kent from birds which heard the approaching Gothas (*Globe*, 12.iii.18). A pair of TAWNY OWLS, in the outskirts of London, were credited with being able to detect the presence of Zeppelins when many miles away; on their approach they appeared to be very angry and nervous, flying from bough to bough (*Daily Mail*, 11.x.16). PEACOCKS are said to have been the first birds to detect the air-raid of May 19th, 1918 (*Daily Chronicle*, 21.v.18).

An observer of an air-raid on the south-east coast on May 20th, 1916, was awakened just before 2 a.m. by the distant approach of sea-planes. NIGHTINGALES were singing lustily, and it was not until the aircraft were right over head that they ceased, not to commence their song again till about 2.30 a.m., when the whirring of the seaplanes had faded into a distant hum. The NIGHTINGALES' reiterated song seemed like a choral defiance to the Huns and was swelled by countless other little British songsters, together with a CUCKOO, who added a jeering call to the retreating enemy alien who so closely resembled that parasitic avian intruder into homes not his own (*Observer*, 28.v.16). Air-craft, however, do not seem, on the whole, to have had much effect on birds, and SKYLARKS have often been seen singing unconcernedly around aeroplanes and airships in the sky. Mr. Charles Dixon, writing of the daylight raid on London on July 7th, 1917, when a fleet of twenty "Taubes" appeared like magic in a sun-bathed sky, states that the effect on bird life was practically nil. Although many German machines passed over him and gun fire was incessant for nearly two hours, he noticed that THRUSHES were singing on and off throughout the raid period, while

Sufferings of Birds

SPARROWS were quite unconcernedly hopping about the roads not a hundred yards from where shrapnel was bursting, and PIGEONS and STARLINGS were equally undisturbed. As regards raids by night, the same competent observer gave his opinion that they caused no disturbance whatsoever among roosting birds (*Manchester Guardian*, 29.xi.17). During the air-raid of May 19th, 1918, a NIGHTINGALE was heard, in a London suburb, singing at the top of his voice when the guns were most clamant and above the crash of a bomb (*Daily Express*, 21.v.18).

Other writers consider that birds were much upset by night raids, and it is recorded that the DUCKS on the lakes in the London parks rose and flew in despair, and that for hours afterwards a lighted window attracted them, with dolorous cries, from their weary flight in quest of the waters from which they had blundered (*Daily Chronicle*, 26.ix.17). The only birds which I saw personally during the daylight raid of July 7th, 1917, were London PIGEONS, which evinced the greatest excitement at the general noise, whirling about in flocks in a thoroughly scared manner.

Charles Waterton was of the opinion that all birds would get used to every sound except that of the gun: this opinion has certainly been upset by the observations of bird watchers on the battle fronts. In this country there has not been sufficient continuous gun fire in any one place for the local birds to become accustomed to it, and in this connection it is interesting to note that when, in November 1917, the bells of St. Paul's rang out a merry peal for the "Victory of the Tanks," the PIGEONS in a startled flock rose fluttering in the air; whereas in happier days, when the ringing of the cathedral bells was a daily occurrence, they used to regard it with indifference (*Manchester Guardian*, 29.xi.17). Similarly, when the armistice with Germany was announced at 11 a.m., "French time," on November 11th, 1918, maroons were discharged, cannons fired, and church bells rung in London, much to the perturbation of the PIGEONS which were unaccustomed to any such sounds. The

Sufferings of Birds

noise of gunfire in their immediate proximity undoubtedly had a more or less transitory effect, according to the duration of fire, on certain classes of birds, chiefly WILDFOWL, on the coast. During the bombardment of Yarmouth and Lowestoft in 1915 the birds were driven away in a panic. Anti-aircraft guns in action terrified BLACKBIRDS, which were much disturbed at each detonation and flitted from tree to tree uttering agitated cries. Even SWALLOWS, in their aerial chase, seemed to dart hither and thither more spasmodically than usual. It seems probable that birds, being naturally sensitive to aerial movements, are disturbed more by the concussion of the air than by the actual sound of the explosions (*Daily Mail*, 10.iv.17).

At the Zoological Gardens in Regent's Park only a few birds raised protesting voices during the raids, and still fewer showed any sign of nervousness next morning. During the daylight raids many of the birds sat with their eyes fixed on the sky, and the CRANES were at all times excited by the presence of air-craft, "making a rare clatter," as their keeper said, "but that signified nothing, for they shout their heads off every time a barge passes on the canal" (*Daily Mail*, 22.x.17).

Casualties among birds were of rare occurrence. In the summer of 1916 it was stated that numbers of LINNETS had been found dead near Louth, with the drums of their ears split, and a complete absence of this species was reported from Suffolk and Hertfordshire (*Times*, 4 and 18.vii.16). In view of the fact that birds did not suffer from the reverberation of the guns on the battle-front, the above statement becomes the more remarkable. As the actual result of air-raids an unlucky bird was more than once reported as the only victim, and a CANARY in its cage was the single casualty of an air-raid on King's Lynn (*Bird Notes and News*, vol. vi. p. 79). During the Zeppelin raid on the night of September 22nd–23rd, 1916, a bomb, dropped within twenty yards of a FOWL run, blew all the feathers except one from a COCK's tail. Next day the bird, with truly Gallic *sangfroid*, was strutting about with the one feather sticking out, none the worse for its adventure (*Globe*, 25.ix.16), and possibly feeling extra cock-a-hoop in the knowledge that two of the Zeppelins had been brought down.

Our intrepid airmen at times were tempted to vie with birds in their own element. In the very early days of aviation naval aviators are credited with having shot DUCKS over the marshes, and I know of one case where an airman, out on a trial trip one day from Ramsgate, came across some MALLARD; he gave chase, opened fire at them with his machine-gun, and killed three, which were picked up by a fisherman and brought to the R.N.A. mess, where they formed a welcome addition to Government rations. There is a story, so far back as 1911, of the French aviator Garros having shot with his revolver at an EAGLE which attacked him while flying over the mountains in Spain, when on his way from Paris to Madrid. Louis Noël, of the French Air Service, shot two EAGLES in the air, from his machine, with a shot-gun on the Salonika front (*Ibis*, 1919, p. 324).

Effect of Air-raids and Air-craft

On the Balkan front, in 1916, a French pilot is said to have shot three EAGLES, with his machine gun, in the course of an hour or so. He regarded the EAGLE as not a very fast flyer but a clever aviator, so that he had to "nose-dive," "side-slip," and "do vertical banks" in order to keep in sight of his quarry. On one occasion a British officer, while testing a new machine behind the French lines, was suddenly passed by a flock of WILD GEESE. He promptly started in pursuit and, oblivious of the direction in which they were heading, flew right across the lines at an altitude at which he offered an easy target even to rifle fire. The Germans, however, were apparently so engrossed in watching the performance that they neglected to fire at him. At last the birds, as he got near them, turned and headed back across the lines again, with the result that he returned to his own territory without a shot having been fired at him (*Daily Express*, 25.iv.16).

An airman has told me that birds were not infrequently killed by coming into contact with aeroplanes; for reasons of their own safety, however, and not from their love of birds, airmen tried to give as wide a berth as possible to any flocks of birds they happened to overtake or meet. An EAGLE is reported to have been overtaken and entrapped in the wires of a French aeroplane nearly 5,000 feet above the earth in Macedonia (*Daily Express*, 18.v.18), but the propeller of an aeroplane is well known to be extremely fragile. I have been assured that on one occasion an airman narrowly escaped with his life, the propeller of his machine having been broken by coming into contact with a soaring LARK. One is reminded of the story of George Stephenson and the cow, whose fate, it will be remembered, he did not expect would be shared by the driver of the locomotive.

The effect of searchlights on GULLS has been described as soporific (? hypnotic); in this case it would seem that they rest in the steady beam much as migrating birds rest in the light of the lantern on lighthouse bird-rests. Another observer, however, states that the

Effect of Air-raids and Air-craft

moving searchlights in the Firth of Forth and in Weymouth Bay roused the GULLS to active flight and the hunt for food (*Bird Notes and News*, vol. vii. p. 3).

III—BEHAVIOUR OF BIRDS IN THE WAR ZONES

8—BIRDS ON THE WESTERN FRONT

MY difficulty in collating the notes by eye-witnesses regarding the behaviour of birds on the Western Front has been great, owing to the various aspects of bird life as seen by individual observers. Some of these were trustworthy ornithologists and all were bird-lovers, but it was only to be expected that most of them were interested in the species which they either saw for the first time or which were of comparative rarity in Great Britain. Thus, many of the observations refer to such species as the GOLDEN ORIOLE, CRESTED LARK, ICTERINE WARBLER, and other birds not uncommon in France and Flanders but rare in this country. Some observers write of migration as far as they could witness it in their prescribed range of observation, and many more write of the presence and daily habits of ROOKS,

Behaviour of Birds

CROWS, MAGPIES, HAWKS, SPARROWS, and other birds common alike to us and our European Allies. To compile a catalogue of the lists of birds recorded at the front would serve no useful purpose here, and it has been my endeavour only to draw attention to any change of habit, peculiar trait, or extraordinary behaviour noticed among birds, as attributable in any way to the War. Moreover, such observations as are at my disposal are derived from reports by soldiers confined perforce to but a very limited portion of the front held by the British troops, so that a bird, described as common in one part of the line, might be rare in another.

It is difficult to sum up the effect of the battle on the Western Front on birds. Though bird life has been described as almost normal in the artillery area and up to within a short distance of the trenches, many species must have been banished from areas which had been devastated by the effects of shell fire (*Ibis*, 1917, p. 528). Very few of the familiar garden birds still clung to the flattened villages, and the HOUSE SPARROW seemed to be the only bird that felt thoroughly at home. In the fields the ordinary birds of the season were plentiful and unconcerned, and when the summer migrants arrived they returned to their old haunts in the half-felled orchards and the ruined houses and nested quite happily (*Ibis*, 1919, p. 57). In times of peace, birds have been known to frequent noisy places with marvellous persistency—for instance, it is on record that a PIED WAGTAIL sat on her nest, placed under a railway switch over which trains passed almost hourly, without deserting it; and, as I have already said, Charles Waterton was of the opinion that birds would get used to every sound except that of the gun. It is therefore remarkable that the outstanding feature of all the notes which I have collected is the unanimity with which all observers insist on the remarkable indifference displayed by birds to the noise of battle.

At the beginning of the War it was expected that the battle-fronts would be deserted by all birds except those grim followers of war, the VULTURE, RAVEN, and HOODIE-

CROW, but facts proved these expectations to be entirely wrong. In autumn and winter bird life is never so assertive as in spring and summer, and it is therefore natural that in the earlier months of the first year of the War observations on birds should have been comparatively few. We have also to picture a landscape of shattered trees, and the ground so torn up by shells that there scarcely remained a single blade of grass (*Ibis*, 1917, p. 528), truly an unattractive spot for any species of resident birds. With the return of spring in 1915, however, the increasing number of birds became a subject for comment in many a letter home, and as one writer put it: " He was a cynic who said even the birds are birds of prey " (*Scotsman*, 25.iii.16). With the approach of summer an extraordinary plant growth was reported, doubtless due to the complete pulverisation of the soil by mines and shell explosions and to the large quantities of nitrates and potash released from the explosives themselves. Coltsfoot and lesser celandine in spring had made stars of gold of old shell-holes of the previous year, and, as the season advanced, it would seem that Nature was doing her utmost to heal the ugly scars of war. An erstwhile Scots gardener, now a subaltern and a recipient of the D.C.M., writing to me on July 20th, 1916, described the cornflowers and poppies as "just terrible."

The following letter gives a graphic description of the change of scenery:—"Summer has disguised the desolation of the stricken land. A few months ago all her wounds were lying open; the bare, stunted tree trunks gashed and broken; gaunt, shell-scarred walls and ruined buildings and everywhere the face of the earth torn and disfigured. Long lines of ditches—for a trench is no more than a deep ditch—winding tortuously here and there, crossing and recrossing. Deep shell-holes full of muddy water, shattered carts and farm implements lying neglected. Everywhere stark desolation. Now it is different. To go up the communication trenches is like a ramble down a country lane; tall grass and wild-flowers have sprung up on the sides and parapets so thickly that they almost roof over the trench. In the neglected gardens of the ruined houses the flowers still bloom. The birds are everywhere" (*Globe*, 14.vii.16). Indeed, it appears that birds were possibly more numerous in Northern France and Flanders than before the War, and "No-man's-land" proved an attractive place, in spite of the noise and all the dangers of artillery fire, for thousands of birds to nest and rear their young (H. Thoburn Clarke, in *The English Review*, March 1918). Nor must it be forgotten that the abnormal quantity of insects doubtless formed an attraction to insectivorous birds, and this was particularly noticed as regards SWALLOWS, MARTINS, and SWIFTS (*Country Life*, 7.x.16, p. 399). An observer, in the neighbourhood of Péronne, writes in September 1918 that the battlefields were so close that an evening stroll brought one to places desolate enough to make one wonder whether life of any sort could still exist, but the very desolation seemed to have its attraction, and in the course of a few weeks it was possible to count nearly sixty different varieties of birds within less than two miles of Péronne (*Daily Express*, 27.ix.18).

That birds were indifferent to the noise of battle is, as I have already said, the unanimous opinion of all observers. There can be no question that a considerable portion of the European avi-fauna had an experience of noise quite without precedent. There has been nothing like the gunfire in the world's history, not only for volume but for duration. It is difficult to visualise a modern battlefield; the very ground quakes from the detonation of the monster guns, there are bursting shells, rolling screens of smoke, rifle bullets flying around as thick as clouds of locusts on the veldt, machine guns r-r-r-r-r-ripping in all directions, while great multitudes of soldiers are at deadly grips in a battle-line scores of miles long and many miles deep. Yet the effect on bird life, so far as can be judged, was singularly small, and birds in areas where the gunfire was hottest displayed remarkable ability in adapting themselves to conditions which in pre-war days would have been regarded as impossible (Charles Dixon in *The Manchester Guardian*, 29.xi.17). On more than one occasion the coming attack of poisonous gas was foretold to our soldiers by the birds, who were the first to detect the noxious fumes (*Bird Notes and News*, vol. vi. p. 102), and they do not appear to have suffered from this vile weapon of destruction which was one of the hideous novelties of the War.

"It was the birds," writes an eye-witness who was at Ypres in the summer of 1918, "that gave one the greatest surprise. Probably Ypres has been more shelled than any other place, particularly as regards gas-shells. It was inconceivable that any animal capable of leaving such an apparently inhospitable and dangerous neighbourhood should remain, especially as the night was worse than the day, for then our own guns added to the tremendous racket" (*Observer*, 5.i.19). The roar of the guns was, to the birds, presumably no more than thunder, and when a shell fell near them it was only some new, if startling, natural phenomenon (*Bird Notes and News*, vol. vii. p. 14). Possibly they became callous to the uproar of the fighting-line, because they quickly realised that the destruction was not loosed upon themselves (*Daily Mail*, 11.vi.17). Indeed, one ornithologist was of opinion that birds preferred the noise of battle to the treacherous quiet of peace, when the inhabitants of the countryside have plenty of time to hunt and otherwise annoy them. M. Reboussin has recorded the numbers of birds seen and heard to the north-west of Verdun, notwithstanding the constant artillery duels going on day and night (*Revue Française d'Ornithologie*, November 1916, pp. 81–92); and Dr. Arthur Allan, of Cornell University, speaking at a meeting of the American Ornithologists' Union at Philadelphia in 1916, stated that: "A doctor, attached to an ambulance corps in France, had counted thirty-five species of birds that had built nests in ruins of buildings and trenches abandoned by inhabitants and troops. Artillery fire, which had swept away entire sections of woods, failed to disturb the birds which happened to be building there, and numbers were seen actually building nests under fire. The tree in which one of the birds was making a nest was entirely swept away by a shell, but a bird in a neighbouring tree went right on building" (*New York World*, 7.xii.16). There is a story of a tree, in front of a dug-out, having been uprooted by a shell and replanted in a shell-hole; a little terrified, trembling, but uninjured bird was discovered on its nest in the replanted tree (*Bristol Times and Mirror*, 5.viii.16). The long-continued bombardment of Nieuport seemed to an eye-witness only an inducement and an incentive to the feathered choirs (*Manchester Guardian*, 10.v.16). The following is part of Mr. H. Perry Robinson's description of the terrific artillery prelude of the British assault on the Ypres salient in June 1917: "The sun as it rose was invisible behind the bank of smoke, but it flushed the sky above with red. It was a truly terrible dawn, most beautiful in its terror, and, if ever dawn did indeed come up like thunder, it was this. Then came the greatest miracle of all, for with the rose-flush in the sky the whole bird-chorus of morning came to life. Never, surely, did birds sing so—BLACKBIRD and THRUSH, LARK and BLACK-CAP and WILLOW WARBLER. Most of the time their voices, of course, were inaudible, but now and again in the intervals of the shattering noise of the guns their notes pealed up, as if each bird were struck with frenzy and were striving to shout down the guns" (*Daily News*, 8.vi.17).

The above quotations from the observations of eye-witnesses illustrate the indifference of birds in general to the noise of battle; the following notes testify to the behaviour of individual species:—

A BLACKBIRD built her nest on a siege-gun daily in action on the front and laid four eggs in it, being, as one of the gunners said, "as saucy as she was confident of our protection" (*Daily Express*, 5.v.16). Another BLACKBIRD built its nest in the body of a field-gun which had not been fired for four days, during which period the nest was made and three eggs were laid. Thereafter the gun was fired daily, but the bird laid two more eggs and continued to sit unconcernedly

(*Bird Notes and News*, vol. vi. p. 87). A BLACKBIRD reared its brood in a nest which was built in a hedge only twenty yards from two 9·2-inch guns. The birds, old and young, never seemed to mind the firing of the guns, which shattered glass in windows and tore the tiles off houses fifty yards away (*Scotsman*, 25.vii.17). A BLACKBIRD'S nest with three young birds in it was found in a captured village which had been right in the old German front line. The mother-bird must have sat on its nest during the whole of the preliminary bombardment and the subsequent terrific fighting; everything around the nest was smashed to atoms (*Daily Mail*, 28.vii.16). The day after the Wytschaete Ridge had been taken, June 7th, 1917, a BLACKBIRD was found sitting on a nest containing five eggs, built about 3 feet from the ground, in a communication trench leading to, and about 15 yards from, the original German line. A big mine had been exploded within 120 yards of the spot, making a crater large enough to accommodate a good-sized house, and there were also shell-holes within but a few yards of the nest (*Times*, 16.vi.17). On Whit Sunday, 1918, the trenches round about a willow, in which a BLACKBIRD had its nest, were smartly shelled with 5·9 for an hour or more. The cock-bird's evensong was, however, unimpaired, and seemed, if anything, more melodious (*Observer*, 5.i.19).

A ROBIN was observed to perch persistently upon the bayonet of a French soldier (*Dumfries and Galloway Standard*, 24.v.15), and another ROBIN chose a dug-out for its nesting-place, where it reared its brood of five without disturbance (*Bird Notes and News*, vol. vi. p. 87). A ROBIN's nest was discovered in an old shell-case half concealed among the ivy covering a ruined shed (*Scotsman*, 20.iv.18).

NIGHTINGALES were frequently heard during the intervals of a night's bombardment (*Times*, 11.vi.16), and sang while monster shells were bursting in a town eight miles from the firing-line (*Scotsman*, 9.vii.16). A brood of young NIGHTINGALES was hatched, on the day of the heaviest Hooge bombardment, on the lip of the first-line trench (*Times*,

Behaviour of Birds

2.iii.16). On May 13th, 1915, at 3 a.m. in the garden of a château a NIGHTINGALE began to sing; half an hour afterwards German shells were rained upon the garden incessantly throughout the day. The bird sang without a pause where the shells fell thickest until mid-day, and survived, for next morning he started again as cheerily as ever (*Times*, 2.iii.16). A wiring party, forced to seek refuge in their front-line trench by a sharp burst of artillery fire lasting five minutes, were surprised, ten minutes after, to hear the sweet song of a NIGHTINGALE in an adjoining coppice (*Scotsman*, 16.vi.17). During one of our most furious artillery duels a NIGHTINGALE sang gaily from the shelter of a dwarfed hawthorn, his song sounding strange and eerie between the violent cannonading from our guns. Yet, in spite of the deafening uproar, he never paused in his singing until the dawn came up, lurid and sullen, over the eastern horizon, and the rain descended in torrents. Later on, his mate was found to have a nest in the hawthorn, and was sitting upon her eggs, apparently unmoved by the thunder of the guns. She certainly paid no heed to the movements of the troops as they passed to and fro, close to the nest, busy with their day's work (*Land and Water*, 14.ix.16). An observer in the battle-zone in the valley of the Ancre writes on June 1st, 1918: " Whether in the front line, or in the still noisier belt just in front of the field-guns, the heavier the fire the more exultant the flow of song; and three nights ago, when we stood-to during a barrage in gas-masks in a wood reeking with mustard gas, the NIGHTINGALES still sang undismayed in the branches overhead" (*Manchester Guardian*, 10.vi.18). In May 1917 a NIGHTINGALE, in Ossus Wood, our most advanced position near the St. Quentin Canal, sang particularly well when the machine-guns fired, as if in answer to them (*Ibis*, 1919, p. 68). About June 1917, when preparations were on foot for the great "third battle of Ypres," a party of troops halted in a wood, midway between Ypres—Elverdrighe—Poperinghe, for the usual "ten minutes easy." The wood was well within shell-fire of the enemy and had just received such a sprinkling of poison gas that the men were compelled, as the air was heavily charged with gas-fumes, to wear their respirators. To their amazement a NIGHTINGALE burst into song in the very wood in which they were halted (*Observer*, 19.i.19). An eye-witness speaks of a NIGHTINGALE which sang his spring song of passion in the derelict garden of a shattered nunnery while shells shrieked overhead (*Daily Mail*, 9.v.17); and another observer writes: "The song of the NIGHTINGALE seemed to come all the more sweetly and clearly in the quiet intervals between the bursts of firing. There was something infinitely sweet and sad about it, as if the countryside were singing gently to itself in the midst of all our noise and confusion and muddy work; so that you felt the NIGHTINGALE'S song was the only real thing which would remain when all the rest was long past and forgotten. It is such an old song too, handed on from NIGHTINGALE to NIGHTINGALE through the summer nights of so many innumerable years" (*Bird Notes and News*, vol. vii. p. 14).

GREAT TITS, doubtless of the continental species, could be seen exploring the broken tree stumps, which were the only indication of the site of Thiepval Wood, in spite of 77 mm. shells which were bursting near (*Ibis*, 1917, p. 532).

REED WARBLERS did not even raise their heads out of their nests during the most heavy firing (*Bird Notes and News*, vol. vii. p. 2).

A pair of ICTERINE WARBLERS were building in a lilac bush in Villers Pluich, on May 25th, 1917; but the place got a bad pounding the same evening and the nest was probably destroyed, as it was only a very short distance behind the firing-line (*Ibis*, 1919, p. 65).

Despite the fact that the largest Hun shells were bursting near, a WHITETHROAT remained on its nest, and, although the very air seemed to be filled with a terrifying, tearing crash followed by a long echoing roar, duly reared its brood of four (*Bird Notes and News*, vol. vii. p. 109).

A BLACKCAP sat on her eggs near Ypres

and never even raised her head from her duty when shells burst close by (*Daily News and Leader*, 22.iv.16). Another BLACKCAP trilled its dainty song night after night, and, although the guns were often fired, sang gaily from his perch in one of the saplings that masked one of the guns (*Land and Water*, 14.ix.16). A BLACKCAP'S nest was blown sideways by shells, but the birds rebuilt another nest within 10 feet of the old nest. The three eggs, which formed the complement of this second venture, were white as snow; but both cock and hen, which alternately sat on them, never flinched when under shell-fire (*Bird Notes and News*, vol. vii. p. 1).

While our guns thundered the overture to the battle of Arras, a CHIFFCHAFF sang impatiently not far behind the battle line (*Times*, 3.v.17).

HEDGE SPARROWS were very fond of building their nests in the broken wheels of derelict waggons (*Scotsman*, 16.vi.17).

SWALLOWS flew around the heaps of ruins that represented their former homes, and it was some days before they became reassured and built in the military huts constructed against the battered walls (*Bird Notes and News*, vol. vi. p. 101). SWALLOWS often nested in billets, and a pair placed their nest and reared their brood in a room used as a field dressing-station (*Scotsman*, 25.vii.17). Another pair built their nest in an "Armstrong hut" only sixty or seventy yards from a battery of 6-inch howitzers, which fired at intervals of about three minutes or less throughout the day, and on special occasions all night long. With each discharge the air concussion, quite apart from the crash of the report, caused the hut to rock, indeed almost to jump (*Scotsman*, 30.vi.17). SWALLOWS did not desert their broods in an outhouse when a shell took off the greater part of the roof, and before the day was over they were using the shell-holes as a convenient entrance through which to pass backwards and forwards with food for their young (*Bird Notes and News*, vol. vii. p. 44). A SWALLOW'S nest with five eggs was found in a German dug-out, about $6\frac{1}{2}$ feet from the floor. Every chimney, house, and shed had been levelled by the retreating Germans (*British Birds Magazine*, vol. xi. p. 67). The sites for nesting in the Péronne district were remarkable owing to the absence of buildings. SWALLOWS often used the circular Nissen huts put up for the troops, and were extraordinarily tame and confiding. A wooden porch, erected outside a ruined single-room cottage at Roisel, was used directly it was put up. Another pair made valiant efforts to build their nest under the hood of a R.A. battery lorry; it went out regularly, but the birds carried on building operations on its return and only gave up after two or three days. A pair of SWALLOWS managed to stick their nest against the vertical wall of a windowless room used as an officers' mess; the nest had no sort of support underneath (*Ibis*, 1918, vol. vi. p. 359). In the very heart of a shelled and ruined town SWALLOWS quietly perched on war-telegraph wires, before migrating, as though the turmoil of battle were a thousand miles away (*Illustrated London News*, 25.ix.15). Preparatory to migration the SWALLOWS collected in flocks and might be seen rising in a body whenever a shell struck the roof on which they were perching (*Land and Water*, 14.ix.16).

MARTINS and SWALLOWS flew over and about the trenches even when the Maxims were rattling away, scattering their deadly shower of bullets (*Scotsman*, 11.viii.17). Quite a hundred HOUSE-MARTINS and SWALLOWS used to circle, in the spring of 1918, around the cathedral and adjacent church tower of Ypres. These were daily shelled and hit ; none the less, nest building went on with patience and perseverance, the necessary mud being obtained from very old shell-holes and the canal banks (*Observer*, 5.i.19). At one part of the line HOUSE-MARTINS delighted to build their nests under the cornice, decorated with cupids and flowers, surrounding a wall that was once part of the ballroom of an historic château (*Scotsman*, 16.vi.17).

A SAND-MARTIN'S nest, full of young birds, was found on the exposed side of a German trench captured in July 1918 ; the parent birds, though they had survived a long and severe shelling of the trench before its capture, seemed absolutely without fear (*Scotsman*, 28.xii.18).

Another fine château, that had suffered badly from Boche shells, was deserted except by a few SPARROWS in the drawing-room (*Country Life*, 6.v.16). Every house that had been blown to bits by shell-fire provided an endless choice of fascinating nesting-places for SPARROWS among the chinks of the ruined walls (*Bird Notes and News*, vol. vii. p. 14). Flocks of SPARROWS might be seen to leave a building which had been struck by a shell only to return there within a few minutes (*Scotsman*, 25.iii.16).

Small flocks of TREE-SPARROWS were frequently seen on our wire in front of the craters which divided the German line from ours (*Ibis*, 1919, p. 57).

Wire entanglements attracted CHAFFINCHES, who evidently considered them preferable to brambles (*Land and Water*, 14.ix.16), and more than one nest was found in a tangle of our barbed-wire briars (*Daily News and Leader*, 22.iv.16). CHAFFINCHES could be heard singing on the Somme whenever there was a lull in the almost incessant fire (*Times*, 11.vi.16).

In April 1917 a flock of a few score LINNETS was always on or about a derelict clump of telegraph wires at Epéhy, where shells fell not infrequently (*Ibis*, 1919, p. 61).

STARLINGS never had such opportunity for unmolested housekeeping as in the remains of the poor battered churches (*Bird Notes and News*, vol. vii. p. 14). Flocks would sweep out in a semicircle from some building which had been struck by a shell, and then swing back to it and settle almost before the brick dust had completely cleared away (*Scotsman*, 25.iii.16).

On one occasion a pair of MAGPIES went on building their nest in a wood when the battle was at its fiercest. Suddenly a shell struck the foot of the tree, sending tree and nest high into the air (*Scottish Naturalist*, 1917, p. 139). A MAGPIE was seen to fly to a crater, made by a shell a few seconds previously, and begin to feed on the grubs among the freshly scattered earth (*Ibis*, 1917,

p. 529). In our advance on Péronne a pet MAGPIE was found in the German trenches and was promptly appropriated by its captor. Acting on the adage of "set a thief to catch a thief," a MAGPIE became the devoted guardian of a soldier's tent (*The Sphere*, 29.iii.19).

The attacks on aeroplanes delivered by the JACKDAWS of St. Omer have already been recorded.

SKYLARKS might at times be seen singing over trenches in which two armies were at death-grips, but they always sang in spite of everything (*Daily Express*, 23.ii.17); in fact, the song of the SKYLARK at dawn over "No-man's-land" was as usual as the song of the sniper's bullet (*Daily News and Leader*, 22.iv.16). SKYLARKS could be heard singing on the Somme, well in advance of the large guns, whenever there was a lull in the almost incessant fire (*Times*, 11.vi.16), and they might often be seen soaring to "Heaven's gate" when aeroplanes above were being vigorously shelled by anti-aircraft guns (*Star*, 3.vii.16). As a soldier-poet wrote:

Birds on the Western Front

> Hushed is the shriek of hurtling shells, and hark!
> Somewhere within that bit of deep blue sky,
> Grand in his loneliness, his ecstasy,
> His lyric wild and free, carols a LARK.

But, if only to show the variability of the human temperament, I record the following story of another British Tommy and a LARK: After a day of terrific fighting, when the bombardment ceased, there lay on the battlefield some scores of our dead and wounded. Of a sudden a LARK darted into the sky, pouring forth his joyous lay. "What the 'ell is 'e singing about?" irritably asked a prostrate Tommy (*London Mail*, 28.viii.15).

SWIFTS were quite fearless of the guns, and their screams were strangely appropriate when accompanied by the moan of a shell (*Country Life*, 7.x.16, p. 399). They shrieked overhead, while 15,000 feet above our shrapnel was bursting round an enemy aeroplane (*Daily Mail*, 9.v.17).

The call of the CUCKOO, so reminiscent of the promise of spring, was eagerly awaited by our fighting men, and on the Somme its familiar note was heard whenever the almost incessant gunfire died down (*Times*, 11.iv.16). CUCKOOS were seen within 300 yards of the first-line trenches (*Scotsman*, 16.vi.17).

OWLS, BROWN and LITTLE, were so callous to the racket of shell and rifle fire that they revelled in hawking rats and mice at night, as usual, and proved of inestimable value (*Bristol Times and Mirror*, 21.vii.16, and *Times*, 10.i.17). Often at night, when the guns were active, OWLS slipped noiselessly past, on silent wing, dodging from side to side in the manner peculiar to the species, and keeping clear as far as possible from in front of the muzzles of the guns (H. Thoburn Clarke, in *Land and Water*, 14.ix.16). A pair of OWLS inhabited the ruins of a barn, which also sheltered an anti-aircraft gun, and whenever this was fired the OWLS dashed out, to be mobbed by all the small birds in the neighbourhood (*Land and Water*, 14.ix.16).

KESTRELS manifested an utter disregard for all the noise of war, and might often be seen over "No-man's-land" or sitting on the stakes supporting the barbed wire (*Scotsman*,

25.iii.16). They hovered about all day in the hottest part of the line, not in the least disconcerted apparently when a promising mouse-area suddenly rose in the air in a cascade of black or yellow earth (*Weekly Westminster*, 14.x.16). One pair of KESTRELS had a nest in a "crack" on the side of a slag-heap which was frequently shelled by the Germans. Whenever a shell exploded near their domicile the birds would fly down to some wire entanglements in the vicinity, but they returned as soon as things quieted down, and never deserted their nest (*Star*, 3.vii.16).

STORKS returned unusually early to Alsace in 1916, but the draining of the marshes round Strasbourg drove them nearly all away from that city. They proved as indifferent to the thunder of the guns as any other bird (*Evening News*, 11.iii.16), and returned to old nesting-places on ruined buildings (*Manchester Guardian*, 29.xi.17).

SNIPE and WATERFOWL of all sorts congregated on the flooded craters and the vast expanse of mud and desolation between the lines (*Manchester Guardian*, 29.xi.17), feeding securely in this "No-man's-land"; for no man from either side dare venture from his trench in pursuit, much less stop to pick up a bird he might chance to shoot, for fear of a sniper's bullet (*Daily Express*, 23.ii.17).

COOTS often indulged in a fight on their own account, and paid little attention to the shells which were falling close to them (*Scottish Naturalist*, 1917, p. 139).

MALLARD, resting on pools close to our lines, were not in the least disturbed by the boom of our guns firing over their heads. They flighted regularly to their feeding-ground somewhere within the German lines, and regularly returned in spite of the terrific roar and rattle of the artillery; nothing could make them forsake their resting-ground, although to reach it they had to cross two immense armies engaged in a deadly fight for a strip of ground (*Land and Water*, 14.ix.16). DUCKS paid more heed to the odd rifle-shots of the sniper than they did to the far greater disturbance of the shells; but on one occasion, when a blazing balloon came down close to a river, they appeared very much alarmed for an hour or more (*Field*, 20.x.17).

The SWANS of Ypres were well known to practically nearly every battalion which tasted the fighting in the Ypres salient. In June 1915 the shelling of this area was particularly severe, but the small family of SWANS, which lived in the moat below the ramparts of the stricken city, glided placidly on the water and survived this and the terrible bombardments of the subsequent three years. Great was the excitement among our troops when, in 1917, the SWANS began nesting operations. On one occasion a German shell fell within a short distance of the nest, but the bird which was then sitting took no notice, except that, for a moment, she fluttered from the concussion. The triumph of the parent birds came when, during the fearful fighting of the third battle for the city, two cygnets were hatched (*Daily Mail*, 22.v.18).

A WOODPIGEON nested in a thorn bush between our front trenches and enemy territory. The thistle-choked valley in which the bush stood was under fire from both sides, and actually served as a sanctuary for the birds (*Times*, 11.vi.16).

Round the caricature of St. Martin's Cathedral at Ypres a faithful remnant of civic PIGEONS still, in 1917, told of ancient peace (*Observer*, 12.i.10).

A fair-sized orchard, directly between our lines and the enemy's and frequently swept by both rifle and artillery fire, seemed the favourite promenade for COCK PHEASANTS (*Bird Notes and News*, vol. vi. p. 88). The familiar "chuk-up, chuc-chuc-cup" of a COCK PHEASANT going to roost could be heard nightly in June 1918 in a clump of willows which lay about 50 yards to the rear of the support trenches at Ypres. This clump was daily plastered with a few shells in the vain hope of finding some 18-pounders. Each day, it was expected, would prove the PHEASANT'S last; but no—sooner or later in the evening the Germans would get the same sound advice, "Shuck-up" (*Observer*, 5.i.19). In many places PHEASANTS were conspicuous by their absence; possibly this was due to the wholesale destruction of the woods or to the poaching proclivities of some of our soldiers (*The Field*, 5.v.17, p. 662).

PARTRIDGES fed securely in "No-man's-land." A nest, with fourteen eggs, was found within fifty yards of a battery position; the bird sat close, though 2,000 rounds were fired daily (*Field*, 29.vii.16, p. 186). Near Gouzeaucourt, in a very much shelled area, a PARTRIDGE sat on seventeen eggs; on either side of her nest, and within two yards of it, were "pip-squeak" shell-holes very recently made (*Times*, 22.vi.17). PARTRIDGES were often seen about the line in the La Bassée sector, where they gave good practice for successful rifle and Lewis-gun fire into "No-man's-land" (*Ibis*, 1919, p. 77). A "Minnie" shell was seen to explode in the middle of a covey of PARTRIDGES; such birds as were not hit simply jumped up, lit again, and immediately went on feeding unperturbed.

QUAILS called to each other while shells exploded close to them (*Land and Water*, 14.ix.16), and could be heard calling during "stand-to" just before dawn, in August 1918, in the reoccupied trenches of the old devastated area of the first Somme offensive (*Ibis*, 1919, p. 77).

CORN-CRAKES "craked" regularly, in spite of the fact that "back areas" were being shelled with great persistence (*Scotsman*, 16.vi.17), and were reported as plentiful in the long hay-grass growing round the front-line trenches on the Somme (*Ibis*, 1919, p. 57).

In the farmyards, HENS went on clucking and laying eggs, while huge shells burst all round them (*The Field*, 27.vii.18).

The foregoing extracts from observations by eye-witnesses are but samples of a host of notes on the behaviour of individual birds on our Western Front. One would have expected that the casualties amongst birds would have been very heavy and that hundreds must have been wounded and killed by bursting shrapnel, but their bodies were seldom seen; possibly they were immediately eaten by the numberless armies of vermin which swarmed about the country. After a wood had been shelled by the Germans it was carefully searched to see the effects on wild life, and only a dead PARTRIDGE, a DOVE, two RATS, and a severely wounded MOLE were found. RATS, MICE, BATS, BEETLES, CATERPILLARS, and BUTTERFLIES, even WORMS many inches below the ground, could be found dead by the dozen, after a gas attack, but no adult birds; although any nestlings must, of course, have been suffocated. On one occasion, when the gas attack was particularly severe and before the great white cloud drifted to our lines, the birds were chirping and twittering gaily, the ROBIN trilling his autumn song, and the STARLINGS singing in full chorus in a shattered tree. Then, except for the awful crash of the guns, nature was silent. Yet, when the gas cloud dispersed, all the birds were singing just as gaily as ever, chirping and hunting food as if nothing had happened. Possibly the birds flee before the gas cloud, just as they flee before a bush fire, and return when it is over (H. Thoburn Clarke, in *Land and Water*, 14.ix.16). One observer writes of having seen several SPARROWS suffering from shell-shock (*Bird Notes and News*, vol. vi. p. 91), and two STARLINGS, roaming listlessly over the ground, every now and then staggering as if weak and unsteady on their legs (*Bird Notes and News*, vol. vii. p. 106), may have been similarly afflicted.

Naturally our soldiers took every opportunity they could of having a day's shooting, and any game they might get proved an acceptable addition to their rations; there are also stories of how our cavalry-men, when at rest behind the lines, used to delight in riding down PARTRIDGES. Shooting was one of the principal recreations of the Allied armies after the armistice of November 11th, 1918. The German civilian population had to surrender its firearms of every description when the occupying troops arrived, so that large stocks of sporting guns and cartridges were available in every town and village. On February 3rd, 1919, an Army order was issued prohibiting, in accordance with the local game laws, the shooting of PARTRIDGES; COCK PHEASANTS and WILDFOWL, however, still remained fair game (*Daily Mail*, 7.ii.19).

Birds on the Western Front

More than one article on bird-nesting at the front proved at least the undaunted keenness of our fighting egg-collectors (*vide Country Life*, 6.v.16; *Ibis*, vol. vi. 1918, etc.). It is, however, truly touching that in the midst of their life-and-death struggle our soldiers should have so often found relaxation and comfort in studying and thinking of Nature. I have repeatedly heard that, when in billets, our men were only too glad to forget the horrors of war in comparing notes on birds. The extreme anxiety which was shown by our soldiers over these morsels of life was surprising, seeing that they had set the value of their own at nothing, as things were (*Daily News and Leader*, 22.iv.16). That the War was not all brutal was proved by many acts of Christian charity as well as by numerous kindly actions towards birds. On one occasion an officer of a London regiment stood for half an hour beside a PLOVER'S nest to prevent the eggs being damaged by the troops who were passing the spot (*Daily Sketch*, 17.vi.16). A soldier, conducting a war correspondent round our lines, told him:

"A BLACKBIRD has a nest with four eggs in it in that hole; but I haven't told anyone; they might disturb the bird" (*Daily Mail*, 23.v.16). When the hospital ship *Llandovery Castle* was torpedoed in June 1918, the second officer returned to the sinking vessel in order to save his pet CANARY (*Daily Sketch*, 3.vii.18). It is recorded of the late Lord Lucas that, on seeing a pair of MARSH HARRIERS circling round their nest on his Whittlesea property, he exclaimed to his gamekeeper: "What a sight! probably the only pair breeding in the British Isles. This is the next great thing to the War!" (*Bird Notes and News*, vol. vii. p. 69). A Scottish miner, shortly afterwards killed on the Western front, told a friend: "If it weren't for the birds, what a hell it would be! I watch them singing, and something comes into my throat that makes me almost greet" (*Dumfries and Galloway Standard*, 7.viii.18). Surely "a master bias ... to gentle scenes" predominated, as in the Happy Warrior, among our fighting men.

9—BIRDS ON THE GALLIPOLI, ITALIAN, MACEDONIAN, PALESTINE, AND MESOPOTAMIAN FRONTS

Gallipoli

THE records which I have from battle fronts other than that in France and Flanders are comparatively meagre. The majority of observations take the form of lists of birds common to the locality though rare in Great Britain, and, though of ornithological interest, fail to come under my present purview. The same indifference on the part of birds to the noise of war is always noticed. An officer of the Mediterranean Expeditionary Force writes: "The astounding thing is how little the birds are put out by the crash of shells, columns of dust, clouds of smoke, and the movement of large bodies of troops over the hitherto undisturbed and peaceful domain" (*Saturday Review*, 9.x.15). They appear to have been far more disturbed by the troops everywhere than by the shells (*Zoologist*, 1916, p. 122).

KESTRELS were seen hovering, taking not the least notice of the bursting Turkish shrapnel or the detonation of the heavy naval guns and field artillery covering the advance and filling the firmament with continuous roar (*Saturday Review*, 9.x.15).

GREY SHRIKES, WARBLERS, and LARKS sat perched on the top of bushes, not having been so much upset by the commotion as to quit the place (*Saturday Review*, 9.x.15).

CRESTED LARKS were very common and tame; if a shell burst in the grass or heather where they were, it merely caused them to fly up and utter their call note, and they soon dropped down again (*Zoologist*, 1916, p. 128).

In May 1915 a WHEATEAR'S nest was found in a cleft on the side of a Turkish trench, above "Lancashire Landing." The Turks had only just evacuated the position, so that the birds had not been frightened away by the bombardment nor by the subsequent landing; the female proved to be quite fearless of man. Two pairs of WHEAT-EARS nested, and reared their broods, not far from Krithia, in a bank which was constantly being plastered with bullets and bursting shells (*Country Life*, 8.ii.19).

More than once a shrapnel shell appeared to burst among a flock of birds, but the actual damage done could never be ascertained. On one occasion a sergeant in the R.A.M.C. found a LARK incapacitated from flying by a slight wound in the wing. It was easily caught and kept in an old biscuit tin, where it was fed on crumbs of army biscuit moistened with water. In a few days the wing was healed and the bird released (*Observer*, 2.i.16).

ITALY

The behaviour of the birds on the Italian front has not, as far as I know, provoked any comment.

A PIGEON, which as a chick had been blown out of its nest and had fallen at the feet of a British gunner, was hand-reared and fed by him until it became so attached to his battery that it would not leave. It accompanied the guns through several fights, notably Asiago, the Austrian offensive of June 15th, 1918, where it was gassed, and Montello.

MACEDONIA

STORKS were numerous near Salonika, and one of these birds acquired the habit of meeting our aeroplanes wherever they landed and soon came to be regarded by the pilots as their mascot.

After a terrific tearing and roaring noise of artillery and shot in "the dead of night" there would be a temporary cessation of the duel, when out would come the NIGHTINGALES, right above the guns, perched sometimes only a few yards from them in some bushes, in a ravine where our guns were hidden.

An EAGLE, well looked after and carefully handled, became the pet of a subaltern in the Balkans.

PALESTINE

It was remarked that in Palestine the birds

took little notice of aeroplanes; as an observer puts it, "they created no more alarm than a steam engine in the next parish" (*The Field*, 17.xi.17).

STARLINGS put in an appearance on the first day of the bombardment of Gaza, at the end of October 1917. Their numbers increased as the year went on, and by December there was a flock estimated at half a million, which fed, being often accompanied by flocks of thousands of ROCK-PIGEONS, on the old British camping-ground.

SWALLOWS, both European and Egyptian, were common throughout the autumn, and invariably accompanied mounted troops to catch the insects disturbed by their horses' feet (*Field*, 30.iii.18, p. 447).

Not far from the Wadi Guzzee, a pair of WHEATEARS took up residence, in May 1917, within two yards of a bivouac occupied by a detachment of R.A.M.C. The hen-bird was quite fearless, and would enter her nest whilst men were washing in a basin less than two yards off, without the least sign of alarm (*Country Life*, 8.ii.19).

I have several notes concerning the birds commonly met with in Palestine though rare in this country, but they throw no light on the effect of the War on birds.

MESOPOTAMIA

None of the notes at my disposal on the birds seen on the Mesopotamian front describe any influence or effects of the War on birds, but, since many observers remark on the abundance of bird life, it may be assumed that birds on this front were no less indifferent to the noise of battle than elsewhere.

I have no information regarding the behaviour of birds on the AFRICAN battlefields.

IV—EFFECT OF THE WAR ON BIRDS

10—MIGRATION IN WAR-TIME

A WRITER in *Lectures pour Tous*, in 1916, declared that "the War had changed all the habits of migrating birds." He stated that "the STORKS which make their home in Alsace began to leave that country a full fortnight before war was declared," and attributed this "to the noise of the movement of the German artillery on its way to attack France"! He went on to say: "In normal times nearly all the birds of passage used to pass over France on their way north or south, but the thunder of the guns has changed all this. The route taken by WOODCOCKS leaving England for warmer climes is across the Channel into Brittany, and then by way of the Loire, Charentes, and Landes to the Pyrenees; and as these birds do not have to cross the war zone, they have kept to their old route throughout the hostilities. But their brethren from Scandinavia and Holland, who used to fly by way of the Aisne and the mud lakes of Champagne, now make a long round by sea and do not touch land until they arrive off the coast of Brittany. SNIPE from Russia and Poland wing their way for sunny climes by way of the western coast of the Black Sea to gain the Bosphorus, or else cross Greece and Roumania. German and Danish SNIPE go south by way of Italy, and the THRUSHES escape the shrapnel of the front in France by crossing Switzerland and making for Italy. The WILD DUCKS of the eastern counties of England, which used to fly over the North Sea, have also a horror of battles, and now fly north, then west, and then south again, skirting the coast of Ireland. The calendar of the migrations, which for thousands of generations has been rigorously kept, has since the war become more elastic, and some birds, such as the MARTINS, have renounced their return journey to the north and remain in Tunis rearing their young" (*Daily Express*, 22.iv.16).

Another French zoologist, M. Cunisset-

Carnot, pointed out in 1916 that in places where fighting occurred the birds became greatly disturbed, screeching and flying about in all directions, unable to settle down anywhere, day and night. Among the migratory birds, those which dwell south of the war zone carried out their flight to the warm lands in the customary direction, but began it somewhat earlier than under normal conditions. As regards migratory birds dwelling north of the war zone, they skirted the line of the front and, instead of flying through France, flew through Switzerland and Italy. For example, BLACKBIRDS, which from Germany and Scandinavia fly southward annually in huge flocks through Burgundy, did not appear there. Similarly, no LARKS were seen in October 1915. In Flanders and Holland there were neither marsh nor water birds (*Times, Literary Supplement*, 29.vii.16).

According to the observations of Russian naturalists during the first year of the War, JACKDAWS and ROOKS disappeared, LARKS no longer sang in the fields, and even SPARROWS grew very scarce. The EAGLE, a constant resident in the Carpathians, migrated to the Balkans, and the wild PIGEON disappeared also. Ordinarily, birds in Central Siberia gravitate during the spring from south to north, in Eastern Siberia from south-west to north-east, and in European Russia from south-west to north-west. Since military operations were proceeding exactly in the region of these migratory routes, the flights of birds were powerfully affected, especially those of the STORK and SNIPE. An extraordinary movement of GEESE northwards was reported, and this was attributed to the military operations in progress in Mitau and White Russia, which prevented these birds from settling there; and the same explanation was given for the abnormal number of DUCK which appeared on the River Volkhov. Individual species of birds which ordinarily carry out their migratory flight through Poland appeared on the island of Œsel. In the Tauride province an abundance of every kind of bird was observed in 1915, particularly of those species which migrate through the Carpathians. Those birds whose nests were usually situated in localities affected by the War were perforce compelled to abandon their homes and migrate to other places, thus evoking an increased flight of individual kinds of birds to certain spots (*Times, Literary Supplement*, 29.vii.16).

In the autumn of 1914 large flocks of GULLS were observed off Norfolk, flying in from the North Sea in so wild and erratic a fashion as to suggest that the explosions at sea had disturbed them; their appearance curiously synchronised with reported sea-fights. Unusual flocks of STARLINGS were noticed in Norfolk in September 1914, and their premature migration was attributed to the disturbing factors of battle which had driven them from the continental marshes (*Zoologist*, 1915, p. 392). It was reported, in the summer of 1916, that thousands of small birds, apparently scared many scores of miles from their native homes, took refuge on American liners (*Times*, 4.vii.16); and the presence of a STORK near Carnarvon in July elicited the query as to whether this rare visitor had been driven by gunfire from more usual haunts in Flanders (*Daily Mail*, 10.vii.16). In 1917 it was publicly stated that, as the result of gunfire, sixty kinds of migratory birds had ceased to visit Britain (*Observer*, 24.vi.17); but this statement was soon disputed (*Nature*, 12.vii.17). In 1919 it was suggested that the scarcity of SNIPE in the British Isles, in the past winter, was due to the effect of big-gun firing in the North Sea and elsewhere, which had deflected the direction of their migration (*Field*, 1.ii.19).

In spite of the above assertions I do not believe that migration was seriously affected. Incessant gunfire on certain parts of the coast may have frightened away WILDFOWL from the vicinity, but statistics from Great Britain during the period of the War do not show any marked diminution in our summer visitants. From such reports as are available from the Palestine front it would appear that migration went on uninterruptedly (*Field*, 30.iii.18, p. 447), and a similar state of affairs seems to have existed on the Mesopotamian front and in the zone of our operations in France and Flanders. In any case, it is a somewhat arbitrary assertion to state that certain migration routes were deserted when these very routes are themselves still only problematical.

Such birds as were migrating during the heavy anti-aircraft barrage of September 1917 and whose path across the moon-lit sky led over London, must have been considerably disturbed by the bursting of shells. The raid periods in 1917 coincided with the autumnal migration of such birds as the WHIMBREL, but possibly they "rose to the occasion" or somewhat diverted their course on seeing the barrage from afar, for not a single bird was found whose death could be attributed to a shell splinter. Small birds, if migrating on those nights, would probably be travelling below the barrage, and September would be too early in the year for many GEESE or DUCKS to be on their journey south. Their passage over any bombarded area in October or November would probably be diverted in a similar manner if they encountered a barrage on the way (Mr.

Effect of War on Birds

Charles Dixon in *The Manchester Guardian*, 29.xi.17). So far from thinking that the birds forsook their accustomed migration routes, I believe that they continued to use their aerial highways, undeterred by the thunder of guns, the marching of troops, and the din of battles taking place many hundreds of feet below them.

Perhaps the abnormal amount of insect food on the Western Front may have detained a few of the migratory insectivorous birds which habitually visit us, and it is possible that Italy's intervention in the war may have had some effect on the numbers of the migratory visitants to Central Europe. It has been stated that when the Austrians invaded Italy they destroyed all the "roccolos" so thickly scattered throughout the compartimento of Venetia. They cut down the groves of hornbeam (skilfully planted and netted in such a way as to give no chance of escape to any autumnal migrant when once within the high green walls), liberated the decoy-birds, and razed to the ground the towers in which the "sportsmen" were wont to conceal themselves from their unsuspecting prey (*Country Life*, 1.ii.19). Italian "sportsmen" are apt to kill any bird; her professional bird-catchers, in their "roccolo" decoys, take thousands of LINNETS and insectivorous birds as they enter the funnel of Italy on their annual emigration to Africa. These men being otherwise engaged, Europe may have benefited by having more birds and less insect pests in consequence (*Manchester Guardian*, 10.vii.16). All things considered, I think, however, that I am justified in saying that there is at present no definite proof that the course of migration was seriously affected by the War.

An airman, who must have been an enthusiastic student of migration, made observations regarding the height at which he met with birds when in the air: SWALLOWS, he found, preferred an altitude of 2,000 ft.; WILD DUCK, 5,000 ft.; and flocks of PLOVER were encountered at 6,500 ft. (*Pall Mall Gazette*, 11.xi.16). Pilots and men in observation balloons agreed that they rarely saw birds at a height of more than 3,000 feet; but a

Effect of War on Birds

captain in the R.F.C., about March 9th, 1918, ran into a flock of LAPWINGS at a height of 6,500 feet, over the line at Hulloch near Lens (*Ibis*, 1919, p. 74). Capt. Collingwood Ingram, in his paper "Notes on the Height at which Birds Migrate," gives some interesting figures obtained from airmen on the Western Front:—

LAPWINGS were observed on fourteen occasions at between 2,000 and 8,500 feet, the height in the majority of cases being between 5,000 and 6,000 feet. A flock of five hundred DUCK, or GEESE, was observed, on November 26th, 1915, at about 11,500 feet. Two large birds, possibly CRANES, were met near St. Omer, in August 1917, at 15,000 feet. Birds resembling LINNETS were seen over Bethune, on August 22nd, 1917, at a height of 10,000 feet. About fifty ROOKS, JACKDAWS, or CROWS were noted over Lens, in March 1917, at 6,000 feet, and "six birds about the size of ROOKS" over Arras, at 3,000 feet, on July 10th, 1918. STARLINGS and FIELDFARES (or REDWINGS) were observed at 3,000 feet in March 1917. Some species of SAND-

PIPER was met with over Arras, towards the end of March 1917, at an elevation of 12,000 feet, and other Limicoline birds at 9,500 and 10,000 feet; WHIMBREL were observed at 4,000 feet, and HERONS at between 2,500 and 3,000 feet (*Ibis*, 1919, pp. 321-5). War-time does not offer the most favourable conditions for the solution of the question at what height birds fly when migrating, but the following advertisement was published in February 1919: "Any notes on the flight of migratory birds made in the air would be highly appreciated. Where possible the species, height, and velocity of flight, time of day, and year would add greatly to value. Single or even negative notes would be most acceptable" (*Times*, 11.ii.19). With the return of peace and a more general use of the aeroplane we may expect many interesting facts and discoveries concerning the question of bird migration, which is, at present, quite unsolved.

11—CHANGE OF HABIT IN BIRDS DUE TO THE WAR

I AM not aware of any change of habit in birds actually due to the War, unless indeed their supreme indifference to the noise of battle may be so described. SWALLOWS are reported to have built freely in trees in France when all buildings had been levelled. An eye-witness described a poplar tree, which had escaped being cut down by the Germans in their retreat, in which there were at least half a dozen nests, the lowest being about 10 feet from the ground and others wherever the birds could get a lodgment (*Scottish Naturalist*, 1918, p. 21). The occurrence of such nests is not unknown (*British Birds Magazine*, vol. v. p. 143), though this is the first occasion, as far as I know, that trees have been freely (I can hardy say habitually) used by SWALLOWS for nidification. MAGPIES, in parts of Somme where most of the large trees had been felled, nested in quite small trees (*Ibis*, 1919, p. 59).

It is certainly remarkable that the vibration of gunfire in the vicinity of nests containing incubating eggs did not destroy them, nor even affect the embryos or the young when hatched. I have already mentioned the case of a BLACKBIRD which reared its brood in a nest built in a hedge only twenty yards from two 9·2-inch guns. This is by no means an isolated case, as reference to the preceding notes will show. That anything so sensitive as an embryonic chick should have been able to sustain with impunity the near discharge of a big gun is certainly unexpected, and Nature, in her farseeing wisdom, can scarcely have foreseen the exigencies that would be required of her in this the most terrific war of all time.

The case of the BLACKCAP whose nest had been blown sideways by shells and who laid three pure white eggs in a second nest within ten feet of the old one (*Bird Notes and News*, vol. vii. p. 1) is worthy of remark here, as it is conceivable that this abnormally colourless clutch was the result of the fright which the female had sustained.

It was noticed that SWALLOWS and MARTINS on the Western Front habitually circled more closely than usual to human beings, doubtless attracted in search of the insects disturbed from the tangle of weeds (*Scotsman*, 15.ix.17), and this habit was also noticed in Palestine (*Field*, 30.iii.18, p. 447).

Eye-witnesses in France were impressed by the fact that all live creatures who had experienced the blast from a gun appeared to avoid passing in front of one; birds proved no exception to this rule (*Land and Water*, 14.ix.16).

The powers of mimicry of the STARLING found scope, writes an artillery officer on the Western Front, in the imitation of the three shrill blasts on a whistle used to denote the approach of enemy aeroplanes. "It was great fun," he writes, "to see everyone diving for cover, and I was nearly deceived myself one day" (*Bird Notes and News*, vol. vii. p. 115). A similar story is told of an OWL in the vicinity of the London "Outer

Barrage" anti-aircraft gun-stations. "The beastly bird learnt to imitate the alarm whistle to a nicety," said the gun commander; "on several occasions he turned me out in pyjamas and, when the crew had manned the gun, gave vent to a decided chuckle" (*Evening Standard*, 18.vi.18). The COCKS and HENS of a French farmyard are said to have learned to make a noise exactly like that of a falling "dud" shell, and it would indeed prove a valuable addition to Darwin's instances of domestic instincts if this imitation could be shown to be transmitted as a fixed habit in the HEN's progeny (*Times*, 29.v.16). It is conceivable that birds bred within the battle area and reared amongst all the turmoil of war may have acquired an innate indifference to terrific noises which they may impart to their progeny, successive generations of which might be expected, if wars continue, to become progressively more indifferent to their abnormal conditions. But this conception, which is without any substantiation by experience, has still to be proved.

SEA-GULLS, rendered ravenous by hard

weather, are alleged to have attacked fishermen off Deal while making a record haul of sprats in January 1917: it was only with considerable difficulty that the fishermen were able to keep the GULLS at bay with their oars (*Globe*, 23.i.17). This temerity on the part of the SEA-GULLS can perhaps hardly be attributable to the War, unless, indeed, they were infected with the war fever which pervaded the world.

In the autumn and winter of 1917–18, when energetic attempts were made to plough up more pasture land in this country, motor-ploughs were extensively employed for the purpose. One observer noticed that the GULLS, normally the constant attendants of the horse-plough, did not follow the motor-ploughs, presumably on account of their noise and smell (*Field*, 16.iii.1918, p. 391). Another observer, however, reported having seen hundreds of GULLS following motor-ploughs as unconcernedly as if they had been of the old-fashioned kind (*Field*, 30.iii.1918, p. 447). It is, perhaps, worthy of remark that under the new régime, when it has become possible to plough one day and sow the next, birds (such as GULLS, ROOKS, and PHEASANTS) have not the same opportunity of destroying wireworms and other noxious insects, of which, under the more protracted system of ploughing with horses, they so beneficially availed themselves.

It was not to be supposed that the unqualified success of the institution of "summer time" would in any way affect Nature. PET BIRDS in houses and POULTRY in farmyards utterly ignored the "Willetted watch" (*Observer*, 24.ix.16); but a PEACOCK which had always been in the habit of going to its night rest at 8.40 p.m. is alleged to have retired to bed at 8.40 p.m. (summer time) on the first day of the innovation and to have continued thereafter to do so! (*Daily Express*, 27.v.16).

Mr. William Beebe, in his recently published *Monograph of the Pheasants*, has pointed out that the far-flung influence of the War has granted a fresh lease of life to many species, such as the PHASIANIDÆ, which were jeopardised by the persecution of the plume-hunter and by the spread of mankind into their haunts. Nearer home, probably the greatest effect of the War is yet to be seen as regards birds. I am thinking of the destruction of forests and woods, sacrificed broadcast for national needs. For a generation, at least, nothing but desolate areas will take the places of what were in pre-war days sanctuaries of wild life (*Observer*, 21.iv.18). Already in 1917 an extension of the range of the GREAT SPOTTED WOODPECKER in the Tay area has been attributed to the cutting down of the larger and thicker woods for war purposes, the WOODPECKERS having been driven into the smaller woods which fill many of the more remote glens (*Scottish Naturalist*, 1916, p. 94). Similar changes of habitat, if not of habit, may be expected; all of them due, more or less, to the exigencies of the war. There can be no doubt that the absence of game-keepers from many estates has favoured an increase of "vermin," both four-footed and winged. From many districts it has already been reported that several species of predatory birds, which were in pre-war days comparatively rare or but locally prescribed, have appeared in unusual haunts. Mr. W. Beach Thomas asks: "Is it an accident, or a result of the keeper's absence, that BITTERNS have bred on the east coast during the period of the war?" (*Daily Mail*, 22.i.19). It is to be hoped that the powers conferred on County Councils by our Wild Birds Protection Acts will be utilised to continue any benefits which our rarer birds may have enjoyed owing to the absence of their persecutors during the War. The effects of increased cultivation should, as regards this country, be beneficial not only to graminivorous but also to insectivorous birds; but there is no reason to suppose that any changes of this kind will immediately influence the habits of birds. In any case, it is imperative that the protection of birds, as at present enforced by our Game Laws and Wild Birds Protection Acts, should not be withdrawn, but rather increased, seeing that our best crop protectors are the insectivorous birds.

V—CONCLUSION

12—ORNITHOLOGISTS KILLED IN THE WAR

IN conclusion, a passing tribute is due to those British ornithologists who, with thousands of other valiant soldiers, have given their lives for King and Country. In days to come mankind will be astounded by the grand total of human lives sacrificed in the War. At present we have figures for our own losses, to which we must add the more or less detailed statistics of losses sustained by our allies and our enemies; this vast total will be swelled still further by those who, though they have not fallen in actual battle, have perished as a direct consequence of the War. Shell and bullet, torpedo and gas, are reckoned as some of the weapons of war; accidental explosions, shipwreck, massacres, famine and disease, must be regarded as its contingencies. A Member of Parliament stated early in 1918 that from

Conclusion

ten to twelve millions had been killed, and that forty-four millions had been maimed and shattered in mind and body by the War (*Daily Mail*, 10.v.18).

To give the roll of honour, even if it was possible, of all the British lovers of birds who fell in the War would occupy many pages, but a fairly complete list could probably be compiled from the columns of such publications as *The Field, The Illustrated Sporting and Dramatic News, British Birds Magazine, The Zoologist, The Ibis,* and *Bird Notes and News.* I propose, however, only to record the names of those who were particularly well known on account of their contributions to ornithology, and whose deaths, often in the prime of their lives and at the commencement of promising scientific careers, are therefore the more to be deplored:

C. J. Alexander (October 4th–5th, 1917); Commander Hon. R. Bridgeman (January 1917); Lord Brabourne (March 12th, 1915); Captain Sydney F. Brock (November 11th, 1918); Captain J. C. Crowley (September 11th, 1916); Eric Dunlop (May 19th, 1917); Cap-

Ornithologists killed in the War

tain Leonard Gray (July 31st, 1917); Lieutenant-Colonel H. H. Harrington (March 8th, 1916); Lieutenant-Colonel R. R. Horsburgh (July 11th, 1916); Captain Hon. Gerald Legge (August 9th, 1915); Captain Lord Lucas (November 4th, 1916); Lieutenant-Colonel Aymer Maxwell (October 8th, 1914); Lieutenant L. N. G. Ramsay (March 21st, 1916); Captain F. C. Selous (January 4th, 1917); Colonel Charles Stonham (January 31st, 1916); George Stout (November 13th, 1916); 2nd Lieutenant G. V. Webster (August 4th, 1917); Major H. T. Whitehead (September 26th, 1915); Lieutenant R. B. Woosnam (June 4th, 1915).

The librarian of the Zoological Society of London, H. Peavot (April 21st, 1917), and the assistant librarian of the Linnæan Society, E. E. Riseley (August 1st, 1917), fell in action in France; and I must not omit to record the loss to ornithological art in the deaths of 2nd Lieutenant O. Murray-Dixon (April 10th, 1917) and Frank Southgate (February 23rd, 1916).

Doubtless our enemies' losses in the scien-

Conclusion

tific ranks have been as heavy as our own. If the outcome of this—the world's greatest War—is to be a permanent Peace, it will be as welcome to scientists as to mankind in general: science can only pursue her course by a mutual and international exchange of thought and must always conserve an attitude of mind abhorrent to such brutal acts as wars. Nature, it is true, is at times cruel; we human beings, who are only her creatures, but endowed with generations of education, should strive, puny though our efforts may be, to eliminate her cruelties and cultivate her beauties until she becomes sublime.

We have seen that the birds were indifferent to the noise of battle, and that migration went on uninterrupted by the struggle of mankind. The greeting card of the Royal Society for the Protection of Birds, issued at Christmas 1917, was a picture of a ROBIN sitting on a snow-wreathed identification cross behind the lines; the following verses, which accompanied the picture, form a fitting ending to these Notes on Birds and the War:

Ornithologists killed in the War

A wooden cross alone may show
A hero's grave; but this we know,
   In Summer's warmth and Winter's cold,
   In Autumn, when the leaves turn gold,
   In Spring, when new life bursts from old,
God sends His messengers of love to seek the spot,
And tell us that the hero's grave is ne'er forgot.

PLATE 1.—"An Eagle"... "became the 'pet of a subaltern'" (p. 138).

Frontispiece]

PLATE 2.—" Our Military Pigeon Service . . . grew to large proportions " (p. 5).

PLATE 3.—"The Pigeons were taken by bicyclists in wicker crates to the front-line trenches" (p. 6).

PLATE 4.—"PIGEONS . . proved of the greatest use; particularly when the telegraph and telephone wires had been cut by shell fire" (p. 6).

PLATE 5.—"HOMERS were taken up in aeroplanes and 'tossed' with messages from behind the German lines" (p. 10).

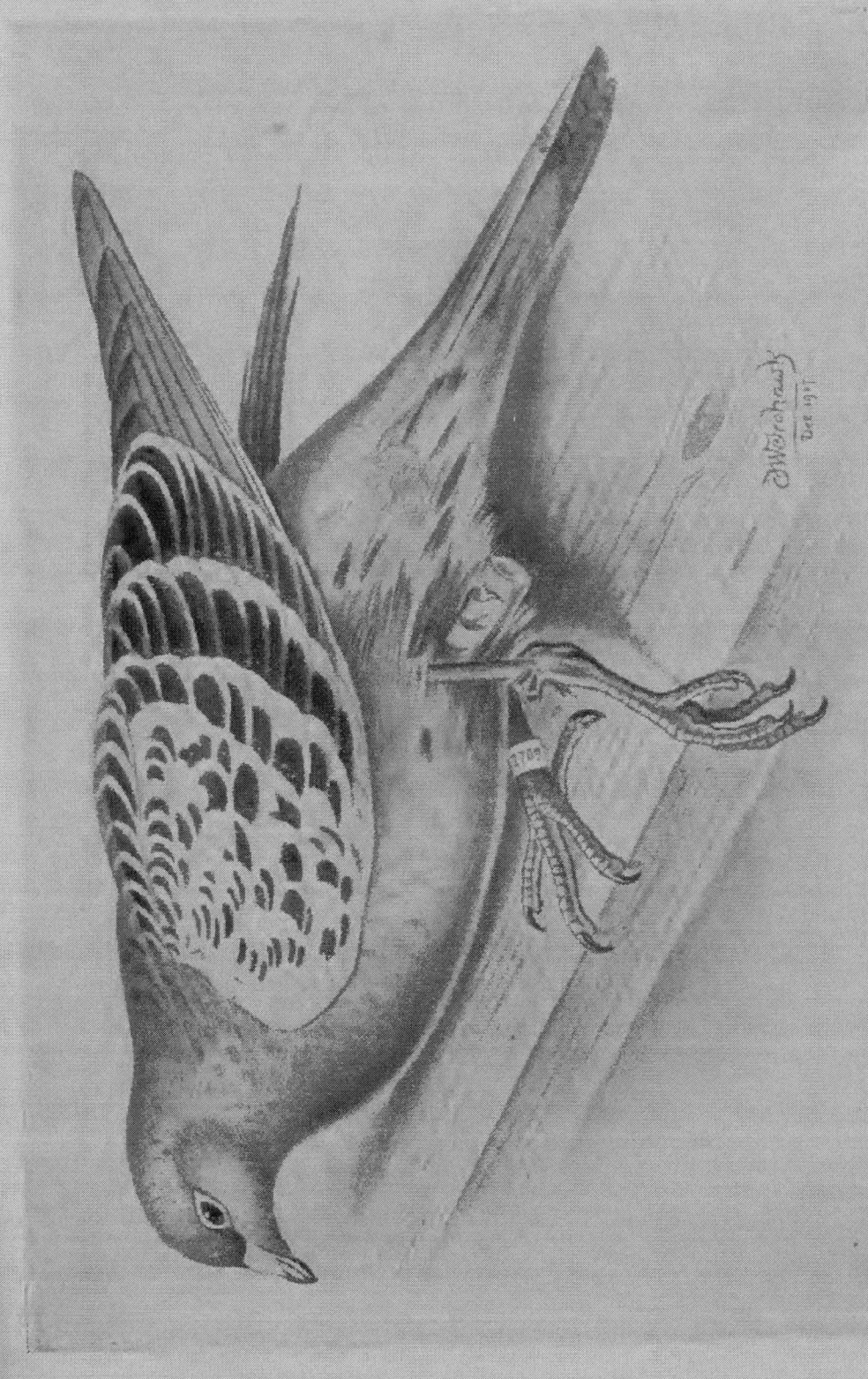

PLATE 6.—"Had the feat of this PIGEON been performed by a human being, it might well have been rewarded by the V.C." (p. 18).

PLATE 7.—"Although hundreds of CANARIES were killed by our shell and gas, those that were rescued . . . were . . . well cared for." (p. 24).

PLATE 8.—" CANARIES were used . . . in ambulance trains to cheer our wounded soldiers with their sweet song" (p. 25).

PLATE 9.—" The first woman gamekeeper" (p. 46).

PLATE 10.—"A wounded soldier ... feeding the GULLS" (p. 69).

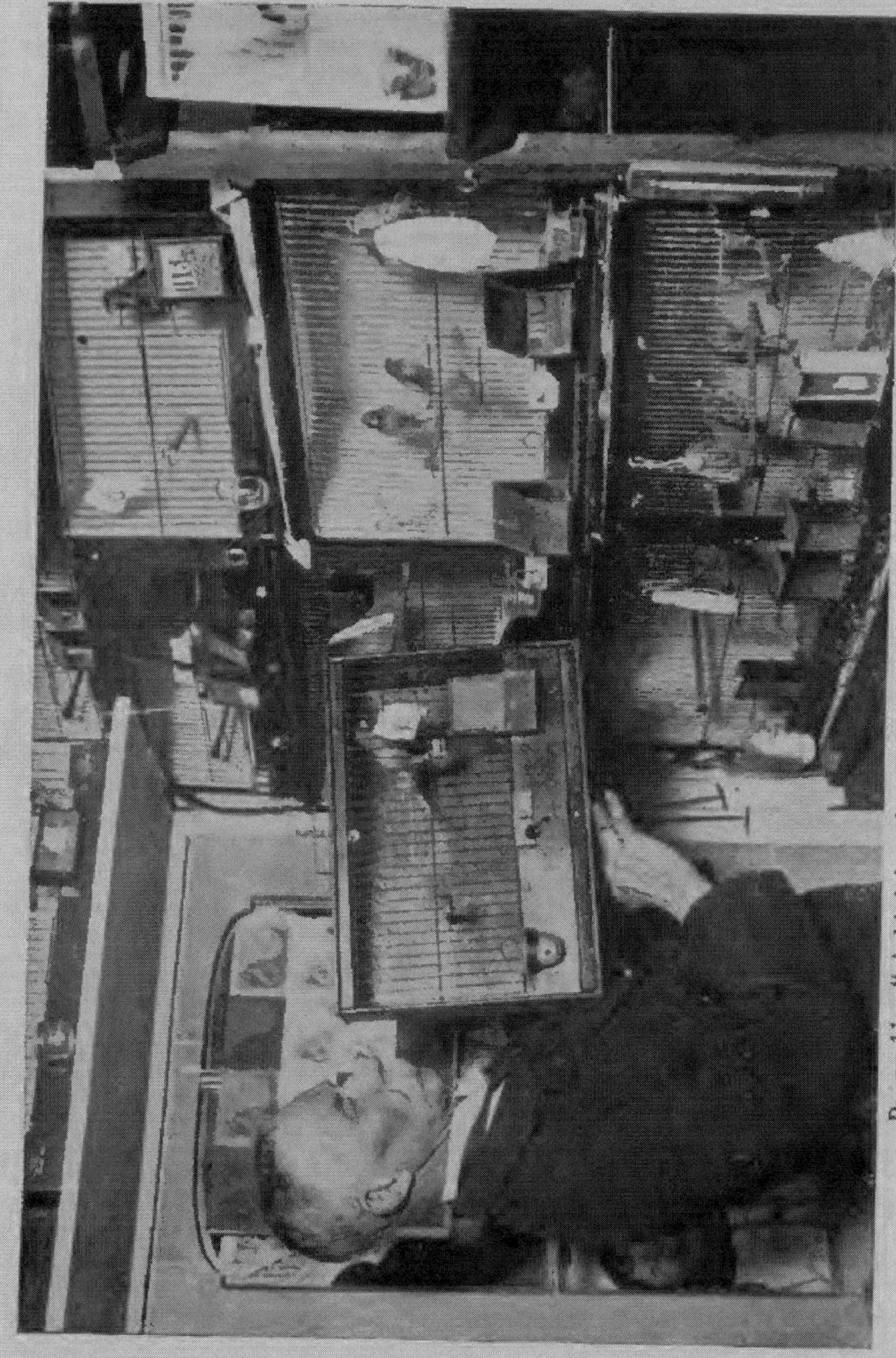

PLATE 11.—"A bird hostel, where soldiers' pet birds were received" (p. 70).

PLATE 12.—" A landscape of shattered trees and the ground so torn up by shells that there scarcely remained a single blade of grass" (p. 102).

PLATE 13.—" To go up the communication trenches is like a ramble down a country lane" (p. 102)

Plate 14.—"Swallows quietly perched on war-telegraph wires" (p. 118).

PLATE 15.—"A pet MAGPIE . . . found in the German trenches" (p. 122).

PLATE 16.—"A PIGEON . . . accompanied the guns through several fights" (p (137)

PLATE 17.—" A STORK ... acquired the habit of meeting our aeroplanes" (p. 138).

Made in the USA
Middletown, DE
10 February 2019